THE SLEEPOVER BOOK

Sleepovers are all about best friends, so this book is dedicated to mine —
• Robin, my sister-by-love, my best friend for thirty years
• Gwodzie, the best "friend in need" our family could ever have
• my writing group — Patricia, Isabel, Judy Ann, Sandra and Tom —
the power of their words has supported me in writing and in life
• and, of course, Phil, Nicole and Teddy Dog, for all the sleepy,
cozy family snuggles we share — M.G.

Kids Can Press acknowledges the financial support of the Government of Canada,
through the BPIDP, for our publishing activity.

Published in Canada by
Kids Can Press Ltd.
29 Birch Avenue
Toronto, ON M4V 1E2

Published in the U.S. by
Kids Can Press Ltd.
2250 Military Road
Tonawanda, NY 14150

www.kidscanpress.com

Edited by Laurie Wark
Designed by Julia Naimska
Printed and bound in Canada by Kromar Printing Limited

The hardcover edition of this book is smyth sewn casebound.
The paperback edition of this book is limp sewn with a drawn-on cover.

CM PA 01 0 9 8 7 6 5 4 3 2 1

Canadian Cataloguing in Publication Data

Griffin, Margot
The sleepover book

Includes index.
ISBN 1-55074-522-0

1. Sleepovers — Juvenile literature. I. Kurisu, Jane. II. Title.
GV1205.G74 2001   j793.2'1   C00-931789-9

Kids Can Press is a Nelvana company

THE SLEEPOVER BOOK

Written by Margot Griffin   Illustrated by Jane Kurisu

Kids Can Press

Contents

INTRODUCTION

YOU ARE HAVING A SLEEPOVER. What could be better than spending the night with your friends? Even preparing for the party is fun. Maybe you will decide on a theme sleepover. Will you be a ghastly greeter for a night at Nightmare Mansion or the director of a music video starring your pals? Imagine all of you at Sleeping Beauties' Spa, doing one another's hair and nails. How about a riotous night spent in tents in your backyard Camp N.B.A. (No Boys Allowed)?

Think of the kitchen fun the gang will have creating pita pizzas or popping Personalized Popcorn. Can't you just picture your buddies all huddled together telling scary stories? How about sneaking around your home trying to solve the mystery of Murder in the Dark?

Your take-home crafts will make your sleepover unforgettable. The fur will fly as you create fuzz-flop Critter Slippers. You will all be ready for the next sleepover with fashions such as Nighty-nightshirts and Boxer Bottoms or Shooting-star Earrings and Moonbeam Friendship Bracelets.

Decide on your guest list, make a plan and haul out your sleeping bag so you and your buddies can party, party, party at your best sleepover ever!

PRE-PARTY PLANNING

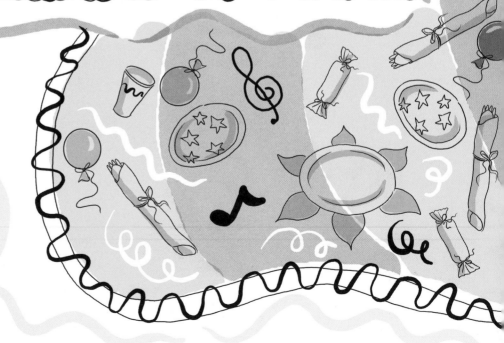

DON'T YOU JUST LOVE TO PLAN A PARTY? This section will give you ideas for making inviting invitations and creating a party mood with just a few fun decorations. By following the instructions for Guest Goodies, you will come up with unforgettable and inexpensive party favors. Plan a theme party, where everything from invitations to decorations and food to fun are coordinated. Follow the suggestions for the '60s Sleep-in, One Magic Night or one of the other theme parties, and your buddies will be talking about your sleepover for weeks afterward.

Party questions

THE BEST SLEEPOVERS are the result of the best plans and the best friends. Be sure to make your family part of your sleepover-planning team and answer these questions together.

Details

★ What is a good date and time?

★ Who is available for adult supervision?

★ How many friends may I invite?

★ What rooms are in or out of the party zone?

★ What time is lights out?

Sleeping quarters

★ Where will my guests sleep?

★ Do I need extra blankets or pillows?

★ Should I ask my friends to bring their own sleeping bags and pillows?

★ Do we need to rearrange furniture and lighting to make sure guests are safe and comfortable?

★ Should Fido or Kitty be kept out of the party area due to a guest's fears or pet allergies?

Food

★ How many meals do I need to plan?

★ Does anyone have a food allergy or special dietary needs (e.g., vegetarian)?

★ What kinds of food will tie into my party theme?

★ Where will we be eating? Are there "No Eating" areas? Is there enough table and chair space?

★ When can we go grocery shopping?

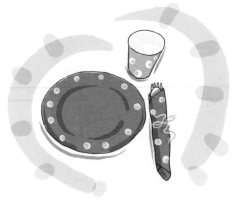

Things to Do Checklist

1. ☆ Make invitations
   ☆ Deliver invitations
   ☆ Follow up with guests who do not R.S.V.P.

2. ☆ Plan menu
   ☆ Write grocery list
   ☆ Shop for groceries

3. ☆ Plan games
   ☆ Gather prizes

4. ☆ Plan crafts
   ☆ Gather supplies

5. ☆ Make or buy guest goodies

6. ☆ Clean my room or party area

7. ☆ Reserve a video
   ☆ Pick it up

8. ☆ Get my own pajamas and sleeping bag ready

9. ☆ Make or buy decorations
   ☆ Put up decorations

10. ☆ Help prepare food
    ☆ Set out food

Invitations

AN INVITATION TO YOUR SLEEPOVER should be fun to get. It gives your guests their first hints about the party. An invitation should include this information:

Who is the invitation for?   Where will the party be held?

Why is the party being held?   What should guests bring?

What kind of party is it?   When will the party begin and end?

How can guests R.S.V.P.?

Bedroll invitation

Unroll this blanketed bundle to discover the party people invitation inside.

You will need:

★ 7 colored Popsicle or craft sticks per invitation

★ roly eyes

★ felt

★ yarn or ribbon

★ a black fine-tip marker, a ruler, glue, scissors

1. Use the marker to print one part of your party information (who, why, what, when, where, bring and R.S.V.P.) at one end of each stick.

2. Glue on roly eyes at the other end of each stick. Position all the eyes differently. Draw a funny mouth, nose, eyebrows and hair.

3. Cut a piece of felt 13 cm x 18 cm (5 in. x 7 in.).

4. Lay the sticks side by side facing down on the felt blanket with the faces peeking above the top. Fold the edge over the first stick and keep rolling until all the stick people are bundled.

5. Cut a 35 cm (14 in.) length of yarn or ribbon. Wrap it around the bundle and tie it in a bow.

6. Write each guest's initials on the outside of a bundle.

Starry invitation

Who could resist an invitation printed on a collection of glittery stars and tucked into a pouch?

You will need:

★ craft paint
★ 7 wood stars per invitation (available at craft supply stores or make them out of bristol board)
★ glitter
★ a dinner plate
★ 2 pieces of different-colored tissue paper
★ metallic cord or ribbon
★ a fine-tip marker, a pen, a glue stick, scissors, a ruler, paper

1. With your finger, rub a thin coat of paint on one side of each star so the wood grain still shows. Let the paint dry.

2. With the marker, print one of each of these words on the painted side of the stars: "Who," "What," "When," "Where," "Why," "Bring" and "R.S.V.P."

3. Flip the stars over and print the corresponding details with pen on the back.

4. Dab a little glue on each star's points. Over a sheet of paper, sprinkle glitter onto the star. Tap the star on the paper so the loose glitter falls off, leaving it on the points only.

5. Place the dinner plate on the tissue paper. Trace and cut out circles of tissue.

6. Place the stars on the circles.

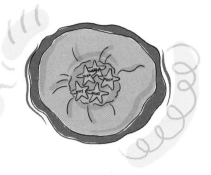

7. Cut two 25 cm (10 in.) lengths of metallic cord. Knot at all ends.

8. Gather the circles around the stars. Wrap the cord around the pouch and tie it in a bow. Fluff out the tissue.

PJ tip If you deliver your invitations individually, instead of in a group, you'll avoid hurting the feelings of friends you can't invite this time.

Decorations

HOW DO YOU MAKE YOUR HOME SAY "PARTY" the minute your friends walk in the door, without spending a lot of time and money on decorations? One way is to concentrate your decorations in one or two areas, rather than spreading them out all over your home. Use party items such as guest goodies and even the food as part of your decorating.

The door to fun

Try some of these welcoming door-decorating ideas for the front door or the door to your party room.

★ Wrap the door in gift paper and add a big bow. Tape on big, bright polka dots or stripes. Hang a bow or a zany stuffed animal from the door knocker.

★ Cover the door with craft paper and write silly party rules that your guests must agree to before entering. Or ask everyone to write a tongue twister or joke as admittance to the party.

★ Put signs on the door such as "PJ Party in Progress," "No Boys Allowed," "People in Pajamas Only," "Caution: Giggle Zone" or "Check Your Snore at the Door."

★ Hang a curtain of streamers from the party-room door.

Table toppers

Whether you are serving a sit-down supper or midnight munchies, set up your table in a way that adds to the party decor. Here's how to jazz up a paper plate.

You will need:
★ a paper plate
★ construction paper
★ a pencil, scissors, glue

1. Trace the plate in the center of a larger piece of construction paper in a coordinating color.

2. Remove the plate and draw shapes such as flower's petals or the sun's rays around half of the circle.

3. Fold the paper in half and cut out your shape.

4. Unfold the shape and glue it to the back of your plate.

Napkin know-how

Add some special folds or ribbon, and these paper napkins double as decorations.

★ Butterfly fold — Fold a napkin back and forth to make a fan. Pinch in the middle and tie with a ribbon or a chenille stem for a butterfly effect. Perch one on each plate.

★ Buffet style — Set a napkin in front of you with an open corner at the top and a closed corner closest to you. Lay the knife and fork on top of each other across the closed corner. Roll them up in the napkin. Tie with a ribbon or secure with a sticker. Tuck into a basket.

Centerpieces

What do you already have at home that would make an interesting centerpiece? Keep your centerpiece low enough so your friends can see one another across the table.

★ Collections — Do you collect dragons, crystals or elephants? Arrange your collection in an interesting way in the center of the table. Create different levels by setting some on mini-boxes, upside-down glasses or books.

★ Guest goodies — Arrange party favors, such as Bottled Goodies (page 16), as a centerpiece.

★ Sprinkles — Scatter jelly beans, confetti or star stickers over your table.

★ Bouquets — Make bouquets from lollipops, pinwheels, fresh or paper flowers.

Guest goodies

IF YOU LOOK FOR BARGAINS OR MAKE THE GOODIES and giveaways yourself, they do not have to cost a lot of money. Here are some fun ideas to get you started.

★ Colorful candies that match your theme — red wax lips for the Sleeping Beauties' Spa party (page 24)

★ Beauty products — bath beads, lip balm or small shampoo samples

★ The write stuff — pencils, notepads, bookmarks or stickers

★ Nail necessities — nail polish, emery board or nail stickers

★ Sporty items — water bottle, small balls or sweatband

★ Hair wear and care — curlers, gel or hair sticks and barrettes made by you (pages 74 to 75)

★ Craft supplies — scented markers, embroidery floss or gimp

★ Jewelry you have made (pages 104 to 111)

Bottled goodies

These cut-down plastic bottles, wrapped in colored cellophane, are perfect for holding anything from bubble gum to bath beads.

You will need:

★ 1 empty 500 mL (16 oz.) plastic bottle

★ tissue paper

★ colored cellophane

★ 2 colors of ribbon that curls

★ a craft knife, a ruler, scissors

1. Have an adult cut the top off the bottle just above the label with a craft knife.

2. Put your guest goodies inside. If something is fragile, put a layer of tissue in first.

3. Cut a 55 cm (22 in.) square of cellophane. Stand the bottle in the middle of the square. Gather the cellophane just above the top of the bottle.

4. Have someone hold the cellophane while you tie two 75 cm (30 in.) lengths of ribbon, one in each color, into a big bow with long streamers. Curl the ends of the ribbon.

T.P. party package

You can turn a cardboard toilet-paper tube into a great party favor.

You will need:

★ 2 pieces of different-colored tissue paper
★ a cardboard toilet-paper tube
★ metallic cord
★ stickers (optional)
★ a ruler, scissors, tape

1. Cut a 22 cm x 25 cm (8½ in. x 10 in.) rectangle from each color of tissue. Lay the two sheets on top of each other.

2. Center the tube on the long side of the tissue. Roll it up snugly and tape closed.

3. Fringe one end of the tissue by cutting strips 1 cm (½ in.) wide to the edge of the roll, all the way around.

4. Tie the fringed end closed with two 25 cm (10 in.) lengths of metallic cord in a double-knotted bow.

5. Tuck your guest goodies in the other end. Fringe and tie off the tissue the same way.

6. Decorate the tissue with stickers matching your theme, if you like.

PJ tip *Use the leftover bottle part to make a Glow Goblet (page 102).*

THEME PARTIES

WHAT'S EVEN MORE FUN than a sleepover? A theme party sleepover! Begin with invitations that hint at the fun to come. Attract aspiring performers to your Video Party with an audition invitation. A registration form for Camp N.B.A. (No Boys Allowed) will have your favorite campers signing up. Keep your decorations simple. Sprinkle star confetti on a blue tablecloth to create the mood for a One Magic Night party. Set the stage for a '60s Sleep-in with flowers or peace posters. Games and activities keep your theme going. Sleeping Beauties' Spa guests will enjoy being pampered with beauty oils they have concocted themselves. Brave Nightmare Mansion guests will have a frightfully good time in your Hall of Horrors. Feed the fun with Personalized Popcorn for the Video Party's Premiere. Toast your Dream Team with Mock Champagne. Treat Camp N.B.A. campers to Microwave S'mores. Design cast T-shirts for your Video Party crew. Stir up sparkly containers of Body Glitter for One Magic Night guests. These Guest Goodies and many more will make your theme party unforgettable.

Nightmare mansion

I DARE YOU TO ACCEPT AN INVITATION TO SPEND THE NIGHT AT NIKKI'S NIGHTMARE MANSION HALLOWEEN PARTY.

If you are brave enough to say yes, come to 1 Main Street at 5:00 P.M. on Saturday

If you survive till morning you may leave at 10:00 A.M.

Be prepared to be scared as you take a haunted house tour, eat ghostly goodies and hear terrifying tales.

Black attire is requested out of respect for the dead who inhabit the house.

BYOC: Bring your own coffin (a sleeping bag will do if your coffin is broken).

R.S.V.P. to Nikki by Friday

Invitation ideas

Create invitations that look as if they have been hidden in a drawer for years. After writing the invitation, crumple it up and open it again. Roll up the invitations, tie them with black ribbon and glue on a fake spider. Deliver your invitations after dark by knocking on the door and then hiding.

Decorations

★ Attach a fake hand to the doorknob and leave the door slightly open so guests can hear the scary music inside.

★ Put signs on the door such as "Enter at your own risk" or "Condemned by Count Dracula."

★ Create black light by purchasing an incandescent bulb at a hardware store.

★ For the table, use fine black yarn to create a spiderweb on a white tablecloth or sheet. Use black paper plates and arrange black candles around a bouquet of dead flowers.

What to wear

★ anything black
★ ghostly white makeup
★ dress up as the Bride of Frankenstein, a mummy, a zombie, a ghost or a vampire

Guest goodies

★ fake spiders
★ skull rings or earrings
★ black artificial fingernails
★ T-shirts that say "I survived a night at Nightmare Mansion"

Menu

★ hard-boiled eyeballs (deviled eggs)
★ ladyfinger cookies
★ Dracula cocktails (cranberry or tomato juice)

Things to do

Scare up some fun by telling scary stories (page 62) and playing Murder in the Dark (page 48), or vary Toilet-paper Pajamas (page 40) by wrapping the models from head to toe as mummies. Guide your friends through this haunted house.

★ A hallway is a good place to set up your Hall of Horrors. Take one guest at a time and leave the others waiting in suspense.

★ Use black light and hang garbage bag strips from the ceiling to tickle guests' faces.

★ Have family members hide behind doors and cackle, scream or jump out as guests pass by.

★ As you guide your guests, tell them the horrific history of the house and have them experience some of these gruesome props.
• monster maggots (a bowl of cold pasta)
• missing relative (bones from the butcher or sticks)
• black widow (rubber spiders)
• broken heart (heart-shaped gelatin)

★ At the end of the hallway, lure them into a room with a coffin where Dracula suddenly sits up and says, "Velcome to Nightmare Mansion. Now leave me alone. I am suddenly feeling very thirsty." (Make a coffin by painting a big appliance box black.)

'60s sleep-in

You are invited to the groovy grand opening of the '60s coffeehouse Claire's Peace Patio, located at 10 Main Street.

Be prepared for a blast from the past by wearing your bell-bottoms and platform shoes.

Festivities begin at 7:00 P.M. on Friday (Claire's birthday!) and end on Saturday morning at 11:00.

A sleep-in will be held to promote the causes of fun and friendship, so bring your sleeping bag. Peace, baby, peace.

R.S.V.P. to Claire

Invitation ideas

Give your invitations flower-power appeal. Print out the invitation on a long, narrow strip of paper. Roll the stip around the stem of a daisy and tie gently with a ribbon. Arrange the invitations in a basket and deliver them personally, wearing your '60s outfit.

Decorations

★ Hang a beaded curtain over the doorway to your coffeehouse.
★ Cover card tables with checked cloths and put candles in empty bottles for a groovy glow.
★ Make posters of happy faces, peace signs and flowers.
★ Set up a stool for poets to read from.
★ Burn incense for that '60s smell.

What to wear

★ bell-bottoms or patched jeans
★ peasant skirts or granny dresses
★ platform shoes or bare feet
★ headbands or flowers in your hair
★ gauzy shirts or tie-dyed T-shirts

Guest goodies

★ anything with '60s symbols, such as peace signs, yin-yangs or happy faces
★ temporary tattoos
★ patches
★ buttons with slogans

Menu

Print up a menu for your coffeehouse, snacks on one side and beverages on the other. Have a friend or big sister play a hippy server by taking the orders.

★ Butterscotch Cloud cookies (page 128) or Sunny Sesame Cherry Bars (page 142)

★ fruit juices or herbal teas with names like "Lemon Love" or "Peace Punch"

Things to do

★ Invite guests to read poetry (a favorite or an original).

★ Ask your parents for some ideas on groovy music to dance to (such as the Mamas and the Papas or the Beatles). If they don't have any, borrow CDs or cassettes from the library.

★ Use your body as a billboard to send out a message of love and peace (see page 82 for body painting instructions).

Sleeping beauties' spa

We don't need a fairy godmother — we can create our own beauty magic. A curling iron and body glitter sure beat a fairy wand and pixie dust.

This coupon entitles you to a night of mutual primping and pampering at Julia's Sleeping Beauties' Spa, located at 7 Main St.

Your appointment time is this Saturday at 7:00 P.M.

You'll go home Sunday at 10:00 A.M. feeling refreshed.

B.Y.O.B.: Bring your own brush. Bring a hair dryer, curling iron, curlers and makeup if you like.

R.S.V.P. to Julia by this Friday

Decorations

★ Put the name of your spa on a big sign on the front door.

★ Choose to decorate a room with lots of electrical outlets and near a bathroom for your spa.

★ Cover card tables with plastic cloths for spa stations for facials, manicures, pedicures and hair play.

What to wear

Make coordinating tablecloths and beauty capes from a roll of plastic table covering. Here's how to make a beauty cape.

You will need:

★ plastic table covering
★ scissors, a ruler

1. Cut a 40 cm x 100 cm (16 in. x 40 in.) piece from the plastic covering.

2. Fold the piece so that two-thirds hangs down the front and one-third down the back.

3. The fold line is your shoulder line. Measure and cut a rectangular hole 15 cm x 18 cm (6 in. x 7 in.) for your head.

Guest goodies

★ sample-sized beauty products, such as nail polish, bubble bath or lotion, in paper lunch bags labeled with the spa's name or in Bottled Goodies (page 16)

Menu

★ fruit smoothies (page 139)
★ fruit kebabs (page 138)
★ Yogurt Sundae Bar Buffet (page 138)

Things to do

★ Decorate one another's nails using tips from page 85.

★ Try some of the hair-raising fun on pages 72 to 79.

★ Follow the instructions on page 86 to make your own scented bath oils.

★ Make Aromatherapy Bundles (page 88) to help you get your beauty sleep.

PJ tip When your spa pals wake up with dark circles and tired eyes, provide relief with soothing cucumber slices and cool tea bags to place on their eyes.

25

Video party

Casting Call

This is your chance to star in a music video.
The famous director Jo-Jo invites you to audition for her latest music video.
You will help choose the music and choreograph the moves.

Auditions and taping will be held from Friday at 7:00 P.M.
to Saturday at 10:00 A.M.
Jo-Jo Video Studio is located at 1 Main Street.

The director likes talent with fresh new looks and plenty of attitude,
so come wearing your most extreme music-video outfit.

Be prepared to rock and roll.

P.S. Bring your pj's and sleeping bag because this is an all-night project.

R.S.V.P. to Jo-Jo

Decorations

★ Put up a sign on the front door with your video company's name. Make a sign for the party-room door that says "Silence Please: Taping in Progress."

★ Put each guest's name on a big, colorful star and tape it to the "dressing room" door. This room needs a mirror and chairs for the stars to sit on.

★ Take lamp shades off lamps to get that bright-light studio feel.

★ Set up a director's chair and use a rolled-paper megaphone.

★ Make a scene slate (handheld chalkboard) for the director's assistant.

Guest goodies

★ sunglasses for all the stars

★ cast T-shirts you've decorated together (see tips for fabric painting on page 95)

★ a copy of the video

Menu

★ for the shoot — dips and dippers (page 132) and a cooler full of bottled water

★ for the premiere — Personalized Popcorn (page 134) and Mock Champagne (page 139) or sparkling fruit juice in fancy glasses

Things to do

★ Choose the music and choreograph the steps.

★ Have a makeup and wardrobe area to transform yourselves into video stars.

★ Rehearse your routine first and then shoot the video.

★ Show the video and celebrate its premiere.

Sleepover theme music

★ Choose your favorite song or a classic with a nighttime theme, such as "Wake Up Little Suzy," by Little Richard; "Rock Around the Clock," by Bill Haley and the Comets; or "Teddy Bear," by Elvis Presley.

One magic night

Star light, star bright. Your future begins tonight.

I predict fun in your future if you accept this invitation
and bring your sleeping bag to my One Magic Night party at
8:00 P.M., July 21, 34 Comet Way.

Come dressed black as night. Horoscopes, fortune-tellers and palm readings
will lift you from the world of today into the world of tomorrow.

R.S.V.P. to your host, Claire Moon

Decorations

★ Decorate with a sun, moon and star theme. Choose a black and gold or a blue and silver color scheme.

★ Use a dark blue tablecloth sprinkled with star- and moon-shaped metallic confetti.

★ Stamp plain paper napkins with star shapes and tie them with thin gold and silver ribbon.

★ Hang Christmas tinsel and foil-covered cardboard stars from the ceiling of your party room.

What to wear

Have your guests make some of these magical accessories to go with their basic black.

★ sparkly garlands for boas or belts

★ Christmas tinsel for shimmery overskirts

★ tinfoil for cuffs, collars, capes, crowns or pin-on stars and moons

Body glitter

Send guests home sparkling with their own containers of body glitter.

You will need:

★ 1 small container per guest (an empty pill bottle or lip balm container)
★ clear hair gel
★ glitter
★ measuring spoons, a toothpick or straw
★ self-sticking labels and a pen

1. Fill the container three-quarters full of gel.

2. Add about 5 mL (1 tsp.) of glitter and stir with a toothpick or straw.

3. Make up a name for your glitter and write it on a label. Include a warning not to apply the glitter gel near the eyes. Stick the label to the bottle.

Menu

★ star- or moon-shaped sandwiches, cut with cookie cutters and garnished with slices of star fruit

★ stardust cake — lay a star stencil on top of a cake, then sprinkle with icing sugar

★ herbal tea made with loose tea in a tea ball, for readings

★ Starry Night Jell-O (page 126)

Things to do

★ Create magical accessories (see "What to wear").

★ Have your mom, a big sister or aunt dress up as a fortune teller and teach your guests how to read palms (page 56).

★ Make Folded Fortune-Tellers (page 57).

FATE

LIFE

HEART

HEAD

29

Camp N.B.A.
(no boys allowed)

To celebrate the beginning of summer holidays, Camp N.B.A. wants you for a camper.

Where: Ling's backyard

When: Gather at dusk on Saturday for roll call. Leave Sunday after chow time

What to wear: White T-shirt + shorts or jeans = camp uniform

What to bring: Pack your camp supplies, including sleeping bag, pillow, water bottle, flashlight and backpack

To register: R.S.V.P. to Camp Director Ling

Decorations
★ A "Welcome to Camp N.B.A." banner will help make your basement or backyard look like camp.

★ Use a picnic table or long table for the dining hall and craft area.

★ Borrow small tents to set up outside. Put a number on each one and assign campers to tents.

★ Set up near a fireplace or mock campfire area. If you have a fire, ask an adult to tend to it.

PJ tip
To tie in with your camp theme, try the Bedroll Invitation on page 12.

Guest goodies

★ a hat or T-shirt you've decorated with the camp name or logo

★ a camp photo taken during the party

★ snack stash packages made by filling plastic bug-proof containers with cookies (pages 128 to 129) — label them with your camp's name

Menu

Call campers to meals by ringing a loud dinner bell and calling out "Chow time!"

★ canteens or water bottles for drinks

★ simple camp food such as hot dogs (or tofu dogs) and beans

★ s'mores and marshmallows roasted in the fire

Traditional s'mores

Generations of campers have enjoyed these deliciously messy treats. Try them and you'll be asking for s'more!

You will need:

★ marshmallows (not miniatures)
★ graham crackers
★ chocolate bars (a plain kind divided into squares works best)

1. Roast a marshmallow over a campfire until golden brown.

2. Layer together a graham cracker, a piece of chocolate and the marshmallow, and top with another graham cracker.

Microwave s'mores

1. On a microwavable plate, layer a graham cracker, a piece of chocolate and a marshmallow.

2. Cook in the microwave on high for 10 seconds or until the marshmallow softens.

3. Top with another graham cracker.

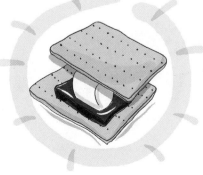

Things to do

★ Take turns telling scary stories (page 62).

★ Challenge each cabin or tent to come up with the funniest song or skit.

★ Make a Dream Catcher (page 98).

★ Have a campfire singsong. Start with "Fire's Burning":

"Fire's burning, fire's burning, draw nearer, draw nearer.

In the glowing, in the glowing. Come sing and be merry."

Dream team sleepover

Let's celebrate the end of the team's season with the best sleepover ever.

We will play together, attend a funny awards banquet and laugh all night long. Everyone will be a winner.

The team will meet at Andrea's Clubhouse (57 Main St.) at 7:00 P.M. on Friday, after the game.

Wear your team jersey and bring your best team spirit.

Don't forget your sleeping bag, pillow and pj's

R.S.V.P. to Andrea

Decorations

★ Make a banner that says "Welcome teammates!"

★ Tie a string across one end of the party room or backyard. Hang a pennant with each guest's name from it.

★ Put up posters of famous team heroes.

★ Create a medal for each team member using a cardboard circle, gold stickers and ribbon.

Guest goodies

★ homemade pennants and medallions
★ a baseball with everyone's autograph
★ water bottles
★ baseball bubble gum
★ sports trading cards

WELCOME TEAMMATES

Menu

This menu is for a baseball team, but with a few variations, you can make it work for a swim team or soccer team, too.

★ Fill large paper cups with popcorn and peanuts in the shell and set in a flat box. Serve them by calling out, "Popcorn! Peanuts! Get your fresh, hot popcorn!"

★ Toast your team spirit with mock champagne (page 139).

★ For the team banquet, serve hot dogs, a cake and coconut ice-cream balls.

★ For your victory breakfast, serve Strawberry Monkey Smoothies (page 139) and Crispy Fruit Rolls (page 143).

★ Ice a slab cake with green icing. Use chocolate bar squares as bases or use chocolate icing to draw the lines for a soccer field. Blue icing, Life Savers candies and gummi fish make a great pool cake.

★ For cool baseballs, roll balls of ice cream in shredded coconut. Store them in a wax paper-lined container in the freezer.

Things to do

★ Play funny team games such as the Radical Relays (page 44).

★ Decorate team caps with silver or gold fabric paint.

★ Invent a team cheer.

★ Hold a funny awards ceremony to honor such achievements as team giggler, most easily embarrassed, team cheerleader, team talker and team joker.

GAMES AND THINGS TO DO

ARE YOU TIRED OF SLEEPOVERS WHERE YOU just sit around and watch videos? With the games in this section, your sleepover will be anything but boring. The action starts at your front door, with a puzzling Team Treasure Hunt. The giggling will begin when your friends play pajama games that have them designing toilet-paper fashions or teaming up for a Pillow Bellies relay. Dim the lights to play Murder in the Dark, or go outside for a sleepover version of Nighty-night Flashlight Tag. If your friends are future rock stars or actors, they will love starring in a music video complete with costumes, choreography and action. Get to know one another better by playing Talk-and-Tell Games or telling fortunes. Take the quiz to find out what kind of pajama-party personality you have. There are so many fun games and thing to do, you won't have time to sleep!

35

Team treasure hunt

A team treasure hunt is a fun way to begin your sleepover and get everyone playing together. The object is for each team to find and unscramble the jumbled words in this sentence: "Friendship is the best treasure of all." The teams, made up of two to four people each, find these words by following the directions on their clue sheets. The teams are then rewarded with treasures. These instructions are for four teams.

You will need:
★ brightly colored bristol board
★ 1 clue sheet per team (see "Clue sheet")
★ treasures (see "Treasures to treasure")
★ scissors, a marker

1. Cut the bristol board into four equal strips. On each strip, use the marker to print the jumbled letters for each word of the sentence in large capital letters. Cut out the seven words from the strip.

2. Place each word in a different location. At each spot there should be a copy of the word for each team. You can place the words in the order they appear in the sentence or mix them up.

3. Give each team a clue sheet.

4. Start each team at a different number on the clue sheet. (For example, Team A could start at clue number 1, Team B at 4 and Team C at 6.)

5. As the teams find the words, they pick up one copy, unscramble the word and go on to the next location.

6. The first team to come up with the complete sentence gets to choose its treasures first.

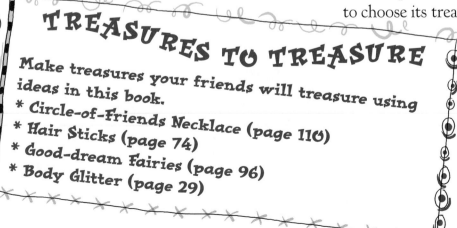

TREASURES TO TREASURE

Make treasures your friends will treasure using ideas in this book.

* Circle-of-Friends Necklace (page 110)
* Hair Sticks (page 74)
* Good-dream Fairies (page 96)
* Body Glitter (page 29)

Clue sheet

You are team _____. Start at clue number _____.

Location	Clue
1. Front hall	Above the shoes, below the hat is where this clue is at.
2. Living room	If a spark could be here, then the clue is near.
3. Kitchen	Behind something wet and round is where the clue is found.
4. Family room	Five steps to the left of the TV is just where this clue will be.
5. Bathroom	Sit on the throne and look back. Now you've got the knack.
6. My room	In the mirror, take a peek, and here is the clue you seek.
7. Backyard	Take seven hops to the right, a clue lurks here tonight.

Unscramble the words and you will see what the best treasure can really be.

Picture perfect

The memory of playing this fun game will last even longer than the photos your friends take.

You will need:
★ 2 instant cameras or other cameras
★ 2 photo assignments sheets (see "Photo assignments")
★ 2 sheets of bristol board
★ tape

1. Divide your guests into two teams. Give each team a camera and a photo assignment sheet. Each team must take all the photos in the assignment by the deadline.

2. The teams can display their pictures by taping them to bristol board.

3. Have each team share its pictures and experiences with the other team.

TEAM-CHOOSING TIPS

You can avoid hurt feelings by choosing team members in these fair ways.
* birthdays in first half of year vs. birthdays in last half
* names in first half of alphabet vs. names in last half
* long hair vs. short hair
* tallest vs. shortest

PJ tip If you make the number of assignments the same as the number of guests, everyone will have a photo to take home.

Photo assignments

Team members take turns taking photos. Here are some sample assignments.

All team members
• in a tub or shower
• dancing outside in their pajamas
• sleeping in or under a bed
• wearing pillows under their pajamas
• in a group hug
• pretending to be a rock group
• posing for the cover of a fashion magazine

CAMERA ALTERNATIVES

If instant cameras aren't available, you can
* set a date for a sleepover reunion when you can share and swap photos
* give each guest a disposable camera at the beginning of the night
* if you write thank you notes to your guests after the party, tuck a party photo into each one

Pajama games

Toilet-paper pajamas

Future fashion designers will have a great time creating toilet-paper pajamas on their giggling models.

You will need:

★ 1 roll of toilet paper per each pair of guests

★ a watch for timing (optional)

1. Ask your guests to choose partners. One partner is the designer, the other the model.

2. See which designer can wrap her model from neck to ankles in toilet-paper pajamas in the shortest time.

3. Have a show of toilet paper-fashions, complete with the models displaying their outfits and the designers doing the commentary.

4. See which pair can unwrap the model the fastest and have the longest strip of toilet paper when finished.

Search me

Your friends will have fun camouflaging an item on themselves and then searching for hidden objects on others.

You will need:

★ 1 small item per person (see "Suggestions")
★ 1 checklist of all the items per person
★ 1 pencil per person

1. Privately give each guest an item and tell her to place it somewhere on herself before returning to the group. The item must be in plain view but camouflaged somehow.

2. When all items are camouflaged, hand out the checklists. Each guest must find out who is hiding which item where and record it on her list. For example, "Star sticker, Nikki, right ear."

3. The first person to locate all items reads her list to the others.

Suggestions

★ an adhesive bandage, a rubber band, a postage stamp, a price tag, a paper clip, a hair ribbon, a bobby pin, a sticker, a safety pin

More pajama games

Getting granny ready for bed

Getting ready for bed is easy, right? Not if you are wearing oven mitts.

You will need:
★ a big nightie, nightcap, slippers, housecoat, a pair of wax teeth (optional)
★ oven mitts
★ a watch for timing

1. Place all the clothes in a pile and put the oven mitts on top.

2. See who can get all of granny's nightwear on in the shortest time — while wearing the oven mitts.

Face-on

Have a camera ready as you watch a blindfolded player put makeup on her partner.

You will need:
★ makeup (lipstick, blush, eye shadow, loose powder)
★ a watch for timing
★ a mirror

1. Ask your guests to choose partners and then sit in a circle. Have the first pair go into the center. Blindfold one partner.

2. The blindfolded player has 2 minutes to make up her friend's face. When the time is up, remove the blindfold and give the made-up partner a mirror. Then reverse roles.

3. Continue playing until everyone is made up and your sides hurt from laughing.

Slipper switch

You can play this ongoing game from the minute your friends arrive until they leave.

You will need:

★ 1 pair of slippers per person (can be fancy or funny)

★ a safety pin or piece of yarn

1. Mark one pair of slippers with a safety pin or a piece of yarn. Put the slippers in a pile or box at the front door.

2. Ask your guests to put on a pair of slippers as they arrive.

3. Throughout the party, when they are least expecting it (while someone is in the bathroom or while eating supper or watching a video), yell, "Slipper switch!" Everybody has to charge around and find someone to switch slippers with.

4. After three or four switches, see who has the pair with the safety pin or yarn. She gets a prize or reward. A new pair of slippers or a pair of Critter Slippers (page 100) made by you makes a great prize.

Radical relays

Makeup madness

This relay has two teams, each cheering on their blindfolded members, who are trying to scoop items into a makeup bag with a spatula.

You will need:

★ 2 empty makeup bags that open at the top
★ cotton balls and tubes of lip balm or gloss (1 item per guest)
★ 2 spatulas
★ 2 blindfolds

1. Each team sits in a circle with a makeup bag in the middle. Spread the makeup items around each bag, and put a spatula beside it.

2. Each team member takes a turn being blindfolded and scooping one item into the bag with the spatula (with her other hand behind her back). The tricky part is that the cotton balls are so light you cannot feel them on the spatula and the round tubes are hard to keep on the spatula.

3. Other team members may shout directions: right, left, forward, backward, higher, lower. The team who gets all the items into the bag first wins and gets to choose their lip balm prizes first.

Pillow bellies

The pillow bellies and balloons in this game are guaranteed to give you belly laughs.

You will need:
★ 1 pillow per guest
★ scarves, belts or string to tie pillows to guests
★ 1 balloon per guest (plus a few extras), blown up almost to the bursting point

1. Ask your guests to choose partners and help each other tie on a pillow.

2. The teams must gently carry the balloons between the partners' pillow bellies — no hands allowed — across the finish line. If the balloon drops to the floor, the partners must pick it up and start over. If the balloon breaks, they are given one more to start again. If they break two balloons, their turn is over.

3. The team that gets an unbroken balloon across the finish line first wins.

Sleeping worms

Wiggles will soon be accompanied by giggles during this wiggle-worm race.

You will need:
★ 2 sleeping bags
★ gummi worms or licorice strings

1. Divide your guests into two teams.

2. When the starter yells, "Go!" the first "worm" on each team jumps into the sleeping bag and wiggles on her belly to the finish line, where she grabs a gummi worm in her mouth, gets out of the sleeping bag and runs back with it to pass to the next player.

3. The first team to collect and eat all its gummi worms and return to the starting position wins.

45

Make a music video

You and your friends dancing and lip-synching to your music, captured on video forever — what could be more fun?

You will need:
- ★ 1 CD or cassette player per cast and a variety of CDs and/or tapes
- ★ a video camera and tapes
- ★ extra batteries
- ★ paper, markers

1. Divide your guests into casts of no more than four each. Challenge each cast to choreograph and perform the moves to a song of its choice. Give each a separate place to rehearse and an hour till show time.

2. Tell the casts that their planning must be complete in half an hour, so they can meet with the videographer and go over their routine. They need to tell the videographer where they will begin and end, which directions they will be facing and what special effects or props they need.

3. Assign each group a time in the last half hour for rehearsing in the taping area.

4. Make sure each cast plans to introduce the group and the individual performers by their stage names. They may also want to make an intro or credits sheet to be included in the taping.

5. Bring all groups to the set for the tapings. Make sure all is "quiet on the set" before beginning.

6. Have a video premiere and watch yourselves perform (see pages 132 to 137 for snack ideas).

7. If you like, tape your guests' post-premiere party as they give their reviews of the performances.

VIDEO POINTERS

If you are shooting the videos yourself, practice ahead of time with the camera so you know how to focus, take wide shots and close-ups. If someone else is your camera person, explain ahead of time how to use the camera and what you want.

Shots — Your videos will be more interesting if you plan a variety of shots.
* wide shot — will show your whole group and the set
* medium shot — use when you move from wide shot to close-up and back
* close-up — use to zoom in on one performer

Timing — Keep each shot to about 8 seconds long.

Angles — Make sure that your videographer and the camera move, so there is a variety of views.

Lighting — The lighting should be directed at the performers' faces. Do not have bright light behind the performers.

Sound — Check beforehand to make sure that the music can be heard from all the spots your videographer might tape from.

Murder in the dark

The wink of death

A wink is the murderer's weapon in this game that can be played in one room.

You will need:

★ 1 playing card per guest, including the queen of clubs

1. Everyone sits in a circle so they can see one another's face. You can dim the lights if you like.

2. Each guest picks a card without showing anyone else.

3. The guest with the queen of clubs becomes the murderer. She murders by winking at another guest without anyone seeing her. That guest counts silently to 5 and then screams and "dies."

4. If no other guest sees the murderer giving the Wink of Death, the murders continue until the murderer is caught.

Murder mystery

Who is the murderer? Who will be the victim? Will the detective solve the case?

You will need:

⭐ 1 playing card per guest, including the jack of spades and the queen of clubs

1. Meet in a room that you can make pitch black with the flick of a switch. Limit play to a few rooms where you have cleared the furniture from the center.

2. Each guest picks a card without showing anyone else. Whoever picks the jack of spades is the detective and whoever gets the queen of clubs is the murderer.

3. The detective is the only one who tells her identity, and she is in charge of turning off the lights.

4. When the lights go out, the detective stands facing the wall with her eyes closed while the game proceeds. All the potential victims walk away from one another. The murderer sneaks up on someone and gives her the Hug of Death (gently, please).

5. The victim counts silently to 5 before screaming and falling down "dead."

6. When the detective hears the scream, she turns the lights on, and everyone goes to the scene of the crime.

7. The detective may ask everyone except the victim questions, such as "Where were you when you heard the scream?" "Was anyone with you?" "Did you see anyone go into the room where the victim was found?" Everyone except the murderer must tell the truth.

8. Conflicting answers will eventually help the detective solve the case. Then get out the cards and start again with a new detective and a new murderer.

49

Out-in-the-dark games

Nighty-night flashlight tag

This version of an old favorite is perfect for a summer sleepover.

You will need:
★ a safe area to play hide-and-seek in the dark
★ a blanket
★ a flashlight

1. Lay the blanket down to be the "bed" (home). Decide who will be It.

2. The player who is It has the flashlight. She lies face down on the bed and counts out loud to 25. The other players run and hide. At 25, It hollers, "Ready or not, here I come!"

3. When It catches a player in her flashlight beam, she chants, "Nighty-night, you're caught in my light," and sends the player to bed.

4. Other players may try to get people out of bed by touching them and whispering, "Wakey-wakey." But if they get caught in the flashlight beam, they must go to bed also.

5. The game is over when all players are in bed. The last one put to bed gets to be It in the next round.

Glowworm hunt

Glowworms glow in the dark, and so will It in this nighttime reverse hide-and-seek game.

You will need:

★ 1 flashlight per player minus one

★ an item of clothing that glows in the dark (see "How does your glowworm glow?")

1. Players decide who is It. It puts on the glow-in-the-dark item, becoming the glowworm, and hides while the others close their eyes and count to 25. Then they begin to hunt in complete silence with their flashlights.

2. When a seeker finds the glowworm, she shuts off her flashlight and quietly joins It in her hiding spot, making sure not to block the worm's glow.

3. The game ends when everyone has joined the glowworm in her hiding spot.

4. The first seeker to find the glowworm is It in the next round.

HOW DOES YOUR GLOWWORM GLOW?

Here are four ways to make a piece of glow-in-the-dark clothing.

* Paint an old T-shirt with glow-in-the-dark paint by following the directions on page 94.

* Stick glow-in-the-dark stickers all over a hat or vest.

* Tie glow-in-the-dark laces around the glowworm's arms.

* Put glow-in-the-dark reflector tape on an old jacket.

Shadow play

Double the fun of traditional shadow play as two partners use their hands and bodies to perform a shadow show.

You will need:
★ 1 slip of paper per person with the name of an animal on it
★ a small bag
★ a light-colored wall (or cover a door or a wall with a white sheet)
★ a bright light (a table lamp set on the floor or a strong flashlight will do)

1. Put the animal names into the bag.

2. Ask your guests to get into pairs and have each person pick an animal name. The partners must create shadows on the wall that portray the animals and perform a short scene between the two animals.

3. Your guests may use their hands and/or bodies. They may team up with another pair.

CAMEL

APE

ELEPHANT

PJ tip Have some hilarious fun by doubling up with your partner to make one big animal shadow. These work best if you start with the biggest partner on the bottom. A moose, an elephant and a giraffe are all shadows you can make with one partner kneeling on the floor and the other one leaning or sitting on her back.

53

Time capsule

Preserve the memories of your friendships and sleepover in this time capsule. You will have fun digging it up and sharing the contents one, five or even ten years from now.

You will need:
★ a large plastic ice-cream container with a lid
★ 1 questionnaire and pen per person (see "Time capsule questionnaire")
★ 1 small personal belonging (a friendship bracelet, a barrette) per person
★ magazines
★ narrow ribbon or yarn
★ a photo of the group or individual photos
★ a kitchen-size garbage bag and tie
★ a shovel
★ duct tape, a waterproof marker, scissors, tape

1. Put a strip of duct tape around the center of the container. Use the market to print the year on the tape and have your guests sign their names.

2. Have each guest fill out a questionnaire and read her answers aloud.

3. Each guest rolls her questionnaire around her personal belonging and a magazine article about her favorite star. Tie these together with a piece of yarn or ribbon.

4. Tape a group photo or individual photos in a collage on the inside of the container lid.

5. Put the lid on and tape it securely with duct tape so no moisture can get in.

6. Put your time capsule in the garbage bag and tie tightly.

7. With a parent's permission, dig a hole and bury your capsule. (Bury it in your closet if you can't use a yard.)

8. Once the capsule is buried, stand over it in a circle, put your right hands together and pledge,

"We promise on the strength of our friendship tonight to return together to this exact spot at this exact time _____ year(s) from now to dig up the capsule and renew our friendships. Our friendships will pass the test of time."

TIME CAPSULE QUESTIONNAIRE

1. Name _____

Age _____

2. My favorite color _____, food _____, teacher _____,

music group _____, movie star _____, book _____.

3. The person I admire the most is _____

because _____

4. I feel good about myself because _____.

5. I want to be _____.

6. The funniest thing that ever happened to me was _____

_____.

7. I predict that (one prediction for each of the other guests) _____

_____

_____

_____

_____

_____

55

Fortune-telling

Palm reading

A future of fun is predicted for your guests if you read one another's palms.

You will need:

★ scented oil or cream (see page 86 for how to make your own oils)

★ 3 washable markers (including a red one for the heart line)

★ fortune-teller accessories — hoop earrings, a scarf to tie around your head, a shawl (optional)

1. Dramatically drop three tiny drops of oil onto your guest's upturned palm while chanting mystically, "One for life, one for head, one for heart."

2. Use the markers to draw and explain these three important lines.

Life line — shows your energy level

• a strong line means you are lively and hyper

• a deep line means you are healthy and calm

• a wavy line means you have both hyper and calm times

Head line — shows how you think

• a straight line means you are a straight thinker and always know what to do

• a wavy line means you don't like to think about one thing for very long

• a faint line means you have trouble even deciding what color of nail polish to wear

Heart line — shows your feelings (the little lines off of it show the number of loves you will have in your life)

• a deep line means you will experience a deep love

• a long line means you will experience a long love

• a broken line means you will be undecided about love

HEART
HEAD
LIFE

Folded fortune-teller

You will need:

⭐ a square piece of paper no smaller than 20 cm x 20 cm (8 in. x 8 in.)

⭐ a ruler, a pencil or pen

1. Fold the paper in half one way. Unfold it and then fold it in half the other way and open.

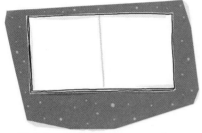

2. Fold each corner to the center point and press the fold with your finger.

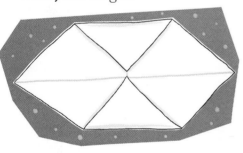

3. Turn the folded paper over and fold each of the four corners to the center.

4. Number the triangles 1 to 8.

5. Lift open these triangles and write a funny answer on each (see "Unpredictable answers"). Close the triangles again.

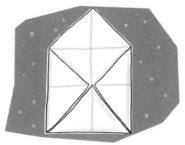

6. Turn the fortune-teller over and print the name of a color on each of the four squares.

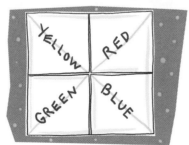

7. Fold the fortune-teller in half to make a rectangle, so the colors are on the outside.

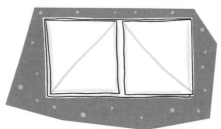

8. Put your thumbs and index fingers under the square flaps and push the points together.

9. Have your friend ask a question that requires a yes or no answer. For example, "Will I become a rock star?"

10. Ask her to pick a color and spell it out as you open and close the points. Then ask her to pick a number. Open and shut the fortune-teller that many times. Ask your friend to choose one of the four numbers revealed inside. Open her flap of choice, and read the answer.

Unpredictable answers

• This is entirely possible, not probable, but possible.

• Only in your dreams.

• How could you even ask that?

• Cannot predict now — only you know for sure.

• From far away in the future, the answer is coming.

• Don't hold your breath waiting for this to happen.

Talk-and-tell games

PENCILS AND PAPER are all you need for these funny guessing games.

Someday/never-ever

From the anonymous written answers, you'll find out whose secret dreams and horrors you are reading.

1. Each guest prepares an answer sheet by writing "Someday" on the top of one half of the paper and "Never-ever" on the other half. Identify each sheet by printing a different letter at the top. Tell your guests they have 6 minutes to fill in the sheet (1 minute per answer).

2. Each player writes down three things she would like to do on the Someday side.

For example, "I will win a Nobel Prize for inventing a cure for cancer." "I will ride a horse without falling off."

3. Each player records three things she would never-ever do, such as "I will never-ever eat liver." "I will never-ever forget my friends."

4. When time is up, gather the answer sheets, shuffle the pile and give each guest a sheet that is not her own.

5. Ask everyone to write the letters used to identify the answer sheets in a column on the back of the sheet. As each friend takes a turn reading out the answers on the sheet she is holding, everyone writes down who she thinks gave those answers beside that letter.

6. Wait until all answers are read before your friends reveal which answers were theirs.

Friendly riddles

These personalized riddles will get your pajama pals remembering funny, scary and embarrassing adventures they have had together.

1. Ask each guest to make up riddles that have each of the other guests' names as the answer. For example, "Who told me I had toilet paper stuck to my shoe?" "Who was with me on the scariest night of my life?" "Who ate a whole pizza with me?"

2. Have each friend take turns reading out her riddles, and see if your friends recognize themselves as the answers.

3. Your guests will probably want to hear more details about these incidents, so share the stories before moving on.

Who's who?

How well do you know your buddies? Your friends may need to interview one another to find out.

1. Fold a sheet of paper into spaces equal to the number of guests you have.

2. In each space, print a funny or interesting fact about each friend that the others may not know (see "Sample game sheet"). Repeat steps 1 and 2 until you have one game sheet for each person.

3. Pass out a game sheet and pencil to each guest. Players must find out who's who by asking questions. For example, "Are you the one who spilled your fruit punch on the principal?" Players may not ask, "Which fact is about you?"

4. When a friend is matched to a fact, have her sign her name in that box on all the game sheets.

5. Everybody wins by getting to know one another better when you share the details of the fact.

Sample game sheet

• fell in the toilet at a boy's birthday party	• met a movie star
• ate worms when she was a baby	• won an inventor's award
• brushed her teeth with hair gel	• wants to be an author when she grows up
• went to school with the back of her skirt tucked into her tights	• fastest runner in our class

Story games

Story web

Here's a cooperative game that will get your friends caught up in the fun of storytelling.

You will need:

★ a stuffed animal, toy or other prop
★ a ball of yarn

1. Tie a funny, embarrassing, magical or scary prop to the end of the yarn. Let's say you use a stuffed frog.

2. Have your guests sit in a circle. As the webkeeper, you start the story with a sentence that ties in with the prop. Try something like, "One morning, I went to plop down on my regular seat on the bus, and there was a frog sitting there looking up at me."

3. Unravel some yarn and pass the prop to a guest across the circle, holding on to the ball yourself. She adds the next sentence to the story and passes the prop to someone else in the circle, holding on to her part of the web. As each teller takes a turn she holds on to her part of the web.

4. Each player helps the story and the web grow. As the webkeeper, you listen for a good time to end the story and announce that the next guest will be the official "ender" who must finish the tale.

5. Stand up with the ball of yarn and ask all guests to stay seated and to keep holding on to the web until you come to roll up the ball.

6. Select a new webkeeper. Let her choose a prop to tie to the yarn and begin weaving another tale together.

Story tie-ons

Tie one of these to the end of the yarn, and your friends won't be able to wait for their turn to weave it into the story web.

• rubber spiders, snakes, toads
• a Pegasus, unicorn or fairy
• a magazine photo of your group's favorite movie star
• a secret note, wrapped present or treasure box

Good news/bad news

The good news is your friends will love playing this silly story game. The bad news is you won't be able to get them to stop.

1. Have everyone sit in a circle and pick someone to start the story with a good news/bad news scenario. For example, "The good news is my favorite rock star rang my doorbell. The bad news is I am not allowed to answer the door when I am home alone."

2. The next player must move the story along with a good-news solution. For example, "The good news is my wild and crazy Aunt Harriet came up the steps right behind him."

3. The third player counters with a bad-news predicament, and so on, alternating good news and bad news around the circle until the last person ends the story.

Good-news beginnings
- The good news is that my wish for _____ came true.
- The good news is I got new _____.
- The good news is _____ finally noticed me.
- The good news is I finally learned how to _____.

Bad-news beginnings
- The bad news is I woke up with a _____ on my face.
- The bad news is when I bent over, I _____.
- The bad news is I hate my new _____.
- The bad news is my gum is now in my _____.

PJ tip Combine these story games by making a story web following the Good News/Bad News format.

61

Scary stories

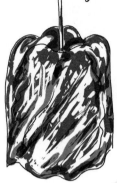

SCARY STORIES ARE BEST TOLD AT NIGHT. Dim the lights and prepare for a fright. Tell this version of the well-known chiller "The Hook" complete with a hook prop, and your friends will be hooked on scary stories forever.

The Hook

It was Jack and Jill's first date. Jill was excited but nervous. It was her first date with someone old enough to drive a car. They went to see the movie *Dracula*. After the show, Jack started driving in the direction away from Jill's house.

Jill said, "Where are we going?"

Jack said, "We are going to Deadman's Cliff. It has a great view of the city at night."

As soon as Jack parked, he turned on the radio, and the broadcast was interrupted by a serious voice. "A killer has escaped from the prison. He was least seen heading toward the city limits. He can be easily identified because he lost his hand in a prison riot and now wears a hook."

Jill shivered. Jack gulped. Jill immediately closed her window and locked her door. Jack hesitated a minute and then did the same. They sat there in the darkness not saying a word.

Finally Jill blurted, "Isn't the prison just north of here? I think I want to go home."

Jack complained, "Ah, come on, we just got here."

"Too bad," said Jill in a brave but squeaky voice. "I want to go home now!"

"Don't be such a wimp, Jill," taunted Jack. "What are the chances of him coming all the way up here? Even if he did, we are safe with the doors locked. He couldn't touch us."

"Use your brains, Jack. One whack from his hook and he could smash this window and open this door. I'm too scared to even talk about it anymore. Take me home — please!"

Jack mumbled something rude under his breath and gunned the engine.

Even over the roar of the engine, Jill was sure she heard the sickening sound of metal being scratched with metal on her side of the car. "Jack, I heard something at my door."

"Not likely," said Jack. That was the last thing he said till the car screeched to a stop at Jill's home.

Jill wanted to get in her safe home as fast as she could. She threw the car door open. Something clanged and banged against the car door and then fell at her feet. It was the hook.

Hook prop

When you say "hook" at the end of the story and stick this hook hand out, your friends will shriek with fear and surprise.

You will need:

★ 1 empty 1 L (32 oz.) plastic bottle
★ a coat hanger
★ scissors or a craft knife
★ tinfoil

1. Ask an adult to help cut the top third of the bottle off. Cut an X in the bottom.

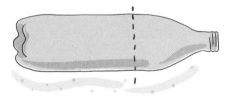

2. Twist the hook end of the hanger around till it breaks off.

3. Shove the straight end of the hook through the X cut, so you can grab it from the inside.

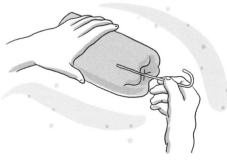

4. Cover the bottle and hook with tinfoil.

Scary story starters

Start your own cooperative scary stories with these beginnings, including your friends in these frightful tales.

★ There were eight girls at the pajama party. Then there were seven. Then there were six. Who would disappear next?

★ Her grandmother made the girls promise never, ever to go down into her basement. One day when she left them alone ...

★ She loved her new room in the daytime. She loved the window seat and her new bed. Everything was perfect until dark. She hated her room at night because ...

★ Where could their friend be? She had been right behind them when they ran screaming out of the cemetery.

Dream on

Dream experts recommend sharing your dreams with a friend to understand them better. So these dreamy activities are planned for partners.

You will need:
★ 1 sheet of lined paper per person
★ 1 pencil per person
★ old teen or celebrity magazines (ask your friends to bring some)
★ scissors

1. Fold each sheet of paper in half. Label one half "P.M. Interview" and the other "A.M. Interview." Write down questions from the suggestion lists on the next page.

2. Each guest cuts out a photo of a star she would like to dream about and puts it under her pillow.

3. Partner up your sleepover pals and give each person an interview sheet and a pencil. Partners take turns interviewing each other to fill in the P.M. Interview questions.

4. Have the interviewers read the answers out loud to the group. Instruct everyone to listen for any words the others may speak in their sleep or watch for motions they may make.

5. In the morning, right after everyone wakes up, the partners interview each other again to fill in the answers to the A.M. Interview questions.

6. Share the answers with the entire group and encourage everyone to contribute words they heard or actions they saw that could tie in with the dreams.

P.M. INTERVIEW

1. Who would you most like to dream about tonight?

2. What would you not like to dream about?

3. Tell me about a dream you have had more than once.

4. How did you feel in that dream?

5. What is the scariest dream you ever had?

6. What is the funniest?

7. Have you ever walked in your sleep? Where did you go?

8. Have you ever talked in your sleep? Do you know what you said?

A.M. INTERVIEW

1. Was the celebrity under your pillow in your dreams last night?

2. Did you dream a dream you have dreamed before?

3. How many dreams can you remember?

4. How did you feel in each dream?

5. What characters were in your dreams? Anyone from the sleepover?

6. Did you talk to anyone in your dreams?

7. Would you like to dream any of these dreams again?

8. Do you think your dreams are different at a sleepover than at home?

Magic tricks

THESE MAGIC TRICKS will cast a spell of fun on your party.

The magical balancing slipper

Why can you balance a slipper on the edge of the table and a guest can't?

You will need:
* ★ a pair of slippers (big, fuzzy animal ones work well)
* ★ a ball of playdough
* ★ masking tape

Before your guests arrive

1. Roll a ball of playdough big enough to fill the toe of the trick slipper without being visible.

2. Test how far out over the table's edge you can pull the heel of the empty slipper before it falls. Mark this fall line on the table with a piece of masking tape.

3. Double check that you can pull the heel of the trick slipper out farther than the masking tape and still have it balance on the edge of the table. Add more playdough if necessary.

Trick time

1. Hold up the two slippers and ask for an assistant from the audience. Give the assistant the plain slipper, and you keep the trick slipper.

2. Demonstrate how your Magical Balancing Slipper can balance over the edge of the table with its toe placed on the masking tape line. Once it is balanced, gently pat the toe of the slipper and say, "Good slipper. Good slipper."

3. Ask your assistant to balance the other slipper. When it falls, graciously pick it up and scold the slipper, "Clumsy slipper. Clumsy slipper." Let the assistant try three times.

4. Console this assistant for her lack of success and ask for a replacement. Never let anyone touch your magic balancing slipper unless you decide to reveal the trick.

What's in a name or a bag?

Your guests will be wowed by your amazing power to pick the right names out of the bag.

You will need:
★ 2 sandwich bags
★ a pen or pencil, paper

Before your guests arrive

1. Print each guest's name on a small piece of paper and fold it half.

2. Place the names of your guests who have birthdays between January and June in one bag. Place the other names (July to December birthdays) in the other bag.

3. Put the January to June bag inside the July to December bag. Smooth the bags so it looks like there is only one bag with all the names inside it. You may need to cut closure parts off.

Trick time

1. Say, "I have amazing mental powers. Each of your names is on one of the pieces of paper in this bag." (Shake the bag.) "As you can see, the papers are folded and I cannot see the names." (Turn the bag around so they can see both sides.)

2. "I will take some names out of the bag and hand them to one of you." (Take all the names out of the inside bag and hand them to a guest.)

3. "Would all the people with birthdays in the months from January to June please stand up?" Ask the guest holding the names to read them out loud. Your guests will be amazed to discover that everyone standing has her name read.

Sleepover quiz

WHAT IS YOUR PAJAMA-PARTY PERSONALITY? It takes all kinds of friends to make a good party. Take the quiz together or individually, then check the scoring to find out what kind of party girls you are.

1. I would invite
a. all the girls in my class
b. my good buddies
c. my best friend

2. The food I would most likely bring is
a. a shopping bag full of chips and candy
b. messy but good brownies I made myself
c. a perfectly arranged veggie platter

3. I would bring this kind of reading material
a. a TV program guide
b. a girls magazine
c. a mystery novel

4. I would wear
a. a big T-shirt and a pair of boxer shorts
b. comfy flannelette pajamas
c. a long nightie

5. I would spend most of my time talking to
a. anybody who will listen
b. my best buddies
c. my host's parent

6. I would spend most of my time talking about
a. anything shocking
b. funny things that we did together
c. my school project

7. If a parent asks, "Who is being so noisy?" it is
a. usually me
b. sometimes me
c. never me

8. During hair play, I might
a. dye my hair purple
b. put a temporary streak in
c. try a new kind of braid

9. My favorite party activity is
a. staying awake all night
b. choreographing our own music video
c. making friendship bracelets

10. My favorite kind of sleepover video is
a. something terrifying
b. something funny
c. something about animals

11. At a sleepover, I am usually
a. the last one to fall asleep
b. up till midnight
c. the first one to fall asleep

12. In the morning, my sleeping area looks
a. like a hurricane blew through
b. messy but comfy
c. just the way I found it the night before

Scoring
If you answered ...

Mostly As — Party animal
You are one wild and crazy partyer. The bigger and noisier the sleepover, the better you like it.

Mostly Bs — Party girl
Just say "Sleepover" and you'll be there, happy to be partying with your pals.

Mostly Cs — Private party person
Your perfect sleepover is with one best friend who enjoys the same quiet activities.

PJ tip

Instead of revealing your answers individually, have each guest cut her quiz into 12 question sections. Number 12 plastic sandwich bags from 1 to 12, and put all the question #1s in bag #1, and so on. Give the bags a shake and read out the results. For example, "For question #1, there were 2 a's, 2 b's and 2 c's." It will be fun to discover your group's similarities and differences.

BEAUTY FUN

DID YOU EVER WANT TO COLOR YOUR HAIR (temporarily, of course) or try a curly, new hairstyle? Well, tonight's the night. A sleepover is the perfect place to try out some beauty fun that you might not dare try anywhere else. Begin by transforming a room into a beauty spa where you can primp and pamper one another. Make glittery nighttime hair accessories, such as a Beaded Braid Wire or phoney Clip-on Curls, and then have a fellow beautician use them to create a new hair look for you. How about trying some Night and Day Nails by being one another's manicurists? After playing hard at being beautiful, you and your sleepover pals can relax together by inventing your own original beauty products, such as aromatherapy bath oils.

Hair coloring

Kool-Aid coloring

This is definitely the most fun you can have with a toothbrush and a package of Kool-Aid.

You will need:

★ a small package of Kool-Aid or other drink crystals

★ 2 mL (½ tsp.) hot water

★ measuring spoons, a small plastic dish, a spoon, a towel, a toothbrush

1. Empty the Kool-Aid into a dish and add the hot water. Stir until the crystals are dissolved.

2. Drape a towel around your shoulders. With dry hair, stand in front of a mirror and plan where you will add the color. You will get the best results if you color sections of your hair, such bangs or a ponytail.

3. Dip the toothbrush into the color and tap off excess drips.

4. Starting from the roots, pull the brush smoothly through a section of hair.

5. Leave to dry for about half an hour. The color will wash out with regular shampooing.

PJ tip

* For variety, use more than one color.
* Make a rainbow by carefully brushing in strips of different colors side by side.
* Go seasonal with orange streaks for Halloween or a red and green ponytail for Christmas.
* Use a narrow hairbrush for wider streaks.

Hairy polka dots

Try this new look that goes way beyond streaking.

You will need:

★ a small package of Kool-Aid or other drink crystals

★ 1 mL (¼ tsp.) hot water

★ measuring spoons, a small plastic dish, a spoon, a towel, a round-ended stencil brush

1. Empty the Kool-Aid into a dish and add the hot water. Stir until the crystals are dissolved.

2. Drape a towel around your shoulders. With dry hair, decide where you want a polka dot and hold that section of hair very flat with your hands.

3. Have a friend dip the stencil brush straight into the color and tap off excess drips. In one firm tapping motion, she dots the color on your hair. She can probably make two dots before adding more color to the brush.

4. Repeat the holding and dotting process all over your head, until it is sufficiently dotty.

PJ tip If you leave the color on overnight, sleep with an old towel on your pillow.

Z Z Z Z Z

Hair accessories

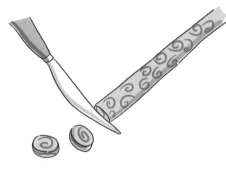

Hair sticks

By turning chopsticks into hair sticks, you can turn a plain old bun or french roll into an exciting hairstyle.

You will need:

★ a pair of chopsticks
★ millefiori Fimo or other polymer clay
★ black gloss enamel craft paint and a paint brush
★ 2 pony beads
★ a ruler, a craft knife, sandpaper, a glue gun

1. Before the sleepover, have an adult use the craft knife to score the chopsticks 17 cm (7 in.) from the end. Break the ends off.

2. Slice two millefiori Fimo slices the thickness of a chopstick. With an adult's help, bake the slices in the oven according to the directions on the package.

3. Sand the ends of the chopsticks smooth.

4. Paint the chopsticks black and let them dry.

5. Glue a pony bead to the uncut end of each chopstick. Glue a baked Fimo slice on top of each pony bead.

6. Crisscross two hair sticks through your bun or stick one down into a french roll.

Starry night barrette

Your hairstyle will sparkle for a special night with this easy-to-make barrette that looks like a mini-constellation.

You will need:
★ gold and silver elastic thread
★ 1 plain barrette base
★ metallic-colored crystal stars
★ scissors, glue

1. Cut two lengths of thread in each color that are four times the length of the barrette base.

2. Double the threads and thread them through the hole in the fastener end of the barrette. Tie the threads into a knot bigger than the hole.

3. Wrap the four strands around the barrette to cover it, but make sure they do not interfere with the fastener. Continue wrapping all the way to the other end and tie off the thread in the other hole leaving tails long enough for a shooting-star look. Knot the end of each thread.

4. Glue two stars over the holes and glue others in a design of your choice.

PJ tip
* Use colored embroidery floss instead of metallic elastic thread.
* Use star-shaped buttons in bright colors instead of crystal stars.
* Make two small barrettes instead of one large one.

75

Buddy braiding

THE BEST BRAIDS happen when you and your best buddies braid one another's hair.

Basic braid

1. Brush your friend's hair into a ponytail and fasten with an elastic.

2. Divide her hair into three sections.

3. Pass the right section over the center section, then the left section over the new center section.

4. Continue braiding this way.

5. Finish by wrapping with another elastic.

Glitter semi-wrap

Choose braid thread that complements your friend's hair color for this spiraling wrap variation.

You will need:

★ a hair clip
★ 1 tiny elastic
★ 2 colors of fine or medium metallic braid thread or embroidery floss
★ a charm or bead (optional)
★ scissors

1. Separate a small section of hair from the hairline or part. Clip the rest of the hair back.

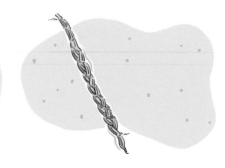

2. Braid the section tightly and secure with a tiny elastic.

3. Cut a strand of each color of braid thread that is twice the length of the braid.

4. Tightly knot one thread, thread A, around the braid as close to the head as possible. Wrap the thread snugly around the braid, leaving even spaces of hair showing. Knot securely around the braid bottom.

5. Tightly knot the other thread, thread B, over the knot of thread A. Wrap thread B around the braid in the center of the sections left uncovered by thread A. Knot tightly over thread A at the braid bottom.

6. Thread a small star or moon charm or bead on to the end of the thread, if you like.

Beaded braid wire

Make bead wires and braid them into one another's hair, or save them to wear to other special nighttime events.

You will need:

★ a spool of 34 gauge metallic craft wire
★ 4 mm gold beads
★ 4 mm silver beads
★ scissors, a ruler, a hairbrush
★ 2 hair elastics

1. Cut a piece of wire the same length as the hair to be braided. Make a 2.5 cm (1 in.) loop at one end, to keep the beads from falling off.

2. Alternately thread gold and silver beads onto the wire until 2.5 cm (1 in.) from the top. Twist a loop in the wire to keep the beads on. Form the end of the wire into a hook.

3. Brush the hair into a ponytail and secure with an elastic. Divide the hair into three sections. Attach the hook of the bead wire to the elastic just above the center section.

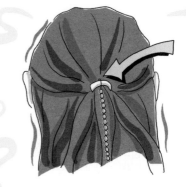

4. Keep the bead wire with this section as you follow the instructions for a Basic Braid (see page 76).

5. At the end of the braid, wrap the bead wire and the braid with another elastic.

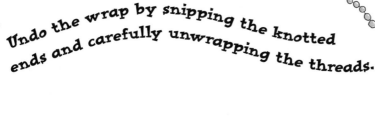

PJ tip Undo the wrap by snipping the knotted ends and carefully unwrapping the threads.

Curling

Clip-on curls

You and your friends will have fun making and wearing these fabulous phoneys.

You will need:

★ 1 small package of curly or wavy doll hair (available at craft supply stores)

★ embroidery floss (in a color similar to the hair)

★ 1 medium-sized barrette

★ scissors, a ruler, a glue gun

1. Cut eight sections of curls, each 15 cm (6 in.) long.

2. Have a friend hold the sections together 2.5 cm (1 in.) from the top.

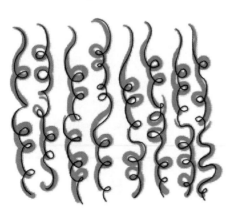

3. Wrap a 10 cm (4 in.) piece of embroidery floss around the curls twice, just above your friend's hand. Tie a double knot.

 PJ tip

* Have the curliest pigtails around by gluing sets of curls to two ponytail holders.
* Glue a cascade of curls to the top band of a haircomb and set it in above a high ponytail.

4. Open the barrette and lay the open side up on your work surface. Put a line of glue under the raised band on the base of the barrette. Slide the tied end of the curls underneath and press down firmly. Let the glue dry.

5. Vary the length of the curls by trimming the outside edges shorter than the middle.

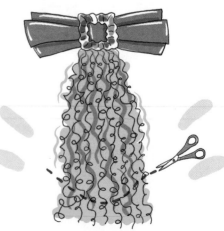

Recycled curls

Don't throw out that tissue paper from your gift bags. One sheet is enough to give you and a buddy heads full of curls.

You will need:
★ 1 sheet of tissue paper
★ styling mousse
★ a blow-dryer or a hairnet or scarf (optional)
★ a ruler, scissors, a comb, a hairbrush

1. Cut the tissue into strips 2.5 cm x 20 cm (1 in. x 8 in.).

2. Massage mousse evenly through your dry hair until it is slightly damp. Divide the hair into 2.5 cm (1 in.) sections with a wet comb.

3. Hold a tissue strip near the bottom of a section and carefully fold the hair up over the tissue.

4. Continue to roll the hair tightly around the tissue. Gently tie the ends of the tissue together to keep the hair in place. Continue to do this until all your hair is rolled up.

5. Blow-dry or cover your hair with a hairnet or scarf and sleep in the curls overnight.

6. When your hair is dry, untie the tissue and carefully unroll each curl.

7. To style, turn your head upside down and gently brush hair into loose curls, or leave them unbrushed and held back with a hairband.

PJ tip For a curly tendril, wrap a small section of well-moussed hair very tightly around the tissue, tie and dry. Unwrap carefully, and do not brush out the ringlet.

Face boosters

WHAT MAKES YOU LOOK YUCKY for 10 minutes and great afterward? A face mask. You and your friends will have fun mixing these beauty concoctions.

Apple-pie pack

This mask helps to dry oily skin. The recipe makes enough for your face and a friend's. You may find it easier to lie back and have a friend apply the mask, rather than do it yourself.

You will need:

★ 1 medium apple
★ 15 mL (1 tbsp.) rolled oats
★ 15 mL (1 tbsp.) half and half cream
★ 15 mL (1 tbsp.) clear honey
★ 2 mL (½ tsp.) cinnamon
★ measuring cups, a paring knife or peeler, a grater, a medium mixing bowl and spoon, a towel

1. Wash and peel the apple. Cut it into quarters and grate into the bowl.

2. Add the oats, cream, honey and cinnamon.

3. Mix well until the mixture makes a paste. Let it set in the refrigerator for 10 minutes. Test by dabbing a fingerful on your face. If it sticks, it is ready. If not, add 2 mL (½ tsp.) of honey.

4. Pat a thin layer of the mixture all over your face avoiding the eye area. Leave on for 10 minutes.

5. Rinse off well using warm water. Gently pat your face dry with a towel. After rinsing off the mixture, run hot water down the drain to prevent clogging. Throw out any leftover mixture.

Pore pickler

You may smell like a pickle, but this toner is removing dirt from your pores. This recipe makes enough to pickle four to six faces.

You will need:

★ 1 medium cucumber
★ 50 mL (¼ c.) white vinegar
★ a sprinkle of spearmint or peppermint flakes (optional)
★ measuring cups, a paring knife, a small mixing bowl and spoon, a grater, cotton balls

1. Peel the cucumber and grate 125 mL (½ c.) into the bowl.

2. Pour in the vinegar.

3. Sprinkle with spearmint or peppermint flakes, if you like. Stir well.

4. Dip a cotton ball into the mixture and dab it on to trouble spots on your face (such as the nose, forehead or chin).

5. Leave it on for 5 minutes and then wash off. Avoid splashing into the eye area.

PJ tip If you want to show your mom how grateful you are for letting you have this great sleepover, pamper her the next day with a mask and toner face treatment.

Body painting

Paint one another with this great-looking neon body paint. Ask your friends to wear an item of white clothing to your party. When you are all painted up, turn on the black light, turn off all other lights, turn up the music and your white clothes and body paint will glow while you boogie.

You will need:
★ hand lotion
★ nontoxic glow-in-the-dark paint (available at craft supply stores) and small paintbrushes
★ measuring cups, paper cups or yogurt containers, a spoon
★ a 75-watt black lightbulb

1. For each color of paint, put 15 mL (1 tbsp.) of lotion into a cup. Add 5 mL (1 tsp.) of paint and stir well.

2. Working with a partner, decide what design you would like (see "Design possibilities") and where you would like it. Stand, sit or lie very still.

3. The painter should start at the top of the design area and work down. Do all parts of one color at a time before moving on to the next color.

Test-patch warning
Try painting a little spot first. If your skin gets itchy or irritated, wash the paint right off and do not apply any more. This paint washes off easily with soap and warm water.

Design possibilities
Choose a design that is simple and has a few basic lines surrounding some solid-colored shapes.

★ Flowering vine — Start with a long, green, wavy line down an arm or leg. Add leaves. Dab pink circular flower centers on. Use a straw or paintbrush to add petals.

★ Snake — A long, wavy, green line winding around your leg with a fat head at one end. Add yellow eyes and a shocking pink tongue.

★ Faces — Paint a happy face on one knee and a sad face on the other.

★ Bracelets and anklets — Paint daisies around your wrist or ankle.

★ Sunshine — Use a straw to dab and draw sunshine yellow rays around your belly button.

★ Gloves — Completely paint your hands for a really funny floating hand effect.

★ Socks — Paint socks or sandals on your feet.

★ Disappearing object — Paint something in the palm of your hand and have it disappear simply by making a fist.

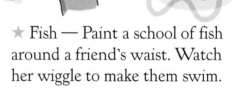

★ Fish — Paint a school of fish around a friend's waist. Watch her wiggle to make them swim.

PJ tip
* Paint peace signs and yin-yangs for the '60s Sleep-in (page 22).
* Paint stars and moons for the One Magic Night party (page 28).

83

Night and day nails

NAIL DOWN SOME FUN by painting one another's fingernails with these night and day designs.

Night nails

You will need:

★ a dark polish (black, purple or deep blue)
★ a silver glitter polish
★ toothpicks
★ newspaper

1. Cover your work surface with newspaper.

2. Paint your nails with two coats of the dark polish. Let it dry.

3. Add star and moon designs to your nails using the silver polish and the point of a toothpick.

Day nails

You will need:

★ a sky blue polish
★ a sunshine yellow polish
★ toothpicks
★ newspaper

1. Cover your work surface with newspaper.

2. Paint your nails with two coats of the blue polish. Let it dry.

3. Have a friend use toothpicks to draw this sunrise and sunset sequence on your nails with the yellow polish.

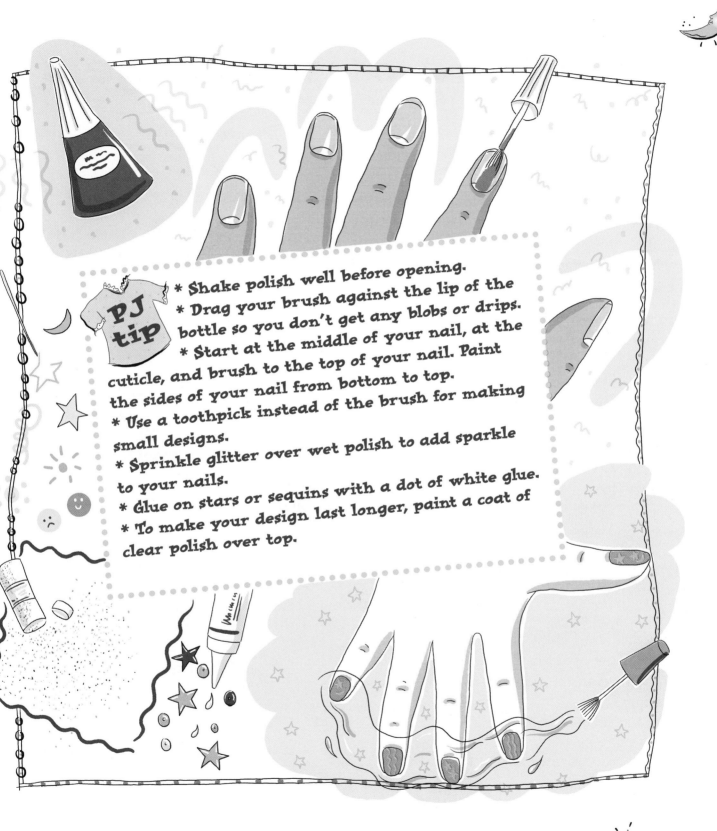

PJ tip

* Shake polish well before opening.
* Drag your brush against the lip of the bottle so you don't get any blobs or drips.
* Start at the middle of your nail, at the cuticle, and brush to the top of your nail. Paint the sides of your nail from bottom to top.
* Use a toothpick instead of the brush for making small designs.
* Sprinkle glitter over wet polish to add sparkle to your nails.
* Glue on stars or sequins with a dot of white glue.
* To make your design last longer, paint a coat of clear polish over top.

Bathing oils and gels

Bath oil

Imagine you and your friends making your own beauty products that smell like a rain forest or a field of strawberries.

You will need:

★ a plastic tablecloth or plastic bags
★ clean, empty plastic toiletry bottles (hotel or sample size)
★ castor oil
★ essential or botanical oils (available at craft supply stores)
★ a small funnel, a piece of paper and a pencil, paper towel, self-sticking labels and a pen

1. Cover your work surface with the plastic tablecloth or plastic bags.

2. Set the funnel in the neck of a bottle. Slowly pour in the castor oil. Fill the bottle about three-quarters full.

3. Add essential oil a drop at a time. After you've added a few drops, shake the mixture and do a sniff test. Keep adding drops until you get the fragrance you want. Write down your fragrance formula so you can duplicate it. For example, 75 mL (1/3 c.) castor oil + 2 drops Moonlight Essence + 4 drops Rain Forest Essence = 1 small bottle of Moonlight in the Rain Forest.

4. Wipe the outside of the cap and bottle to remove all traces of oil.

5. Make up a name for your oil and write it on a label. Include instructions to add a capful per bath. Stick the label to the bottle.

PJ tip
* These little bottles of bath oil make perfect guest goodies for the Sleeping Beauties' Spa party (page 24).
* If you set up a table as a beauty lab, your guests will have fun experimenting and sniff-testing one another's fragrance formulas.

Body glitter gel

Your guests will twinkle and sparkle all night long when they wear this body glitter.

You will need:

★ extra-hold styling gel (the thicker the better)

★ clean, empty flat plastic containers (such as lip gloss, ointment or hand cream containers)

★ glitter

★ a spoon, measuring cups, a tiny spoon or stir stick, paper towel, glue, self-sticking labels and a pen

1. Fill a container about three-quarters full of gel.

2. Add the glitter. You'll need 5 mL (1 tsp.) of glitter for 15 mL (1 tbsp.) of gel.

3. Stir the glitter so it is evenly mixed through the gel.

4. Wipe the outside of the container clean of glitter gel.

5. Cover the top of the lid with glue and dip it in a pile of glitter. Shake off any excess.

6. Make up a name for your glitter and write it on a label. Include a warning not to apply glitter near eyes. Stick the label to the bottle.

PJ tip This is a fun activity for the One Magic Night party (page 28). You can also make containers of glitter gel for each of the stars of your Video Party (page 26).

Aromatherapy bundles

Make one of these mini-sachets to tuck under your pillow, and you will fall asleep to the smell of lavender. Scent another with peppermint to help you face the morning feeling peppy.

You will need:

★ a coffee mug
★ 2 colors of felt
★ polyester fiber stuffing
★ 2 essential oils (see "Nighty-night scents" and "Wakey-wakey scents")
★ narrow ribbon
★ pinking shears or scissors, a pen, a ruler

1. Place the mug on the felt, trace a circle with the pen and cut it out using pinking shears.

2. Roll a piece of stuffing into a ball the size of a large marble. Place it in the felt circle.

3. Scent the stuffing with one drop of a Nighty-night oil or Wakey-wakey oil.

4. Cut a 23 cm (9 in.) length of ribbon.

5. Gather the top of the felt snugly together. You may have to use the top of the pen to tuck the stuffing inside.

6. Have a friend tie the ribbon in a knot and then a bow while you hold the felt together. Trim the ribbon to desired length.

 PJ tip
* You can make your essential oils last longer by diluting them with baby oil.
* Place a bundle on each guest's pillow just before bedtime.
* Make up a basketful of Wakey-wakey bundles to hand out as guest goodies in the morning.
* Make extra bundles for your own backpack, gym bag, locker or sock drawer.
* Tuck a Wakey-wakey bundle into your pencil case to help keep you alert at school.

PJ tip

NIGHTY-NIGHT SCENTS
These aromas will help relax and soothe your tired mind and body: sandalwood, cypress, jasmine, patchouli and chamomile.

WAKEY-WAKEY SCENTS
These aromas will help you feel wide awake and cheerful: ginger, grapefruit, lemon, lime and rosemary.

CRAFTS

YOUR SLEEPOVER PALS WON'T BE ABLE TO RESIST creating these nighttime crafts made with gold and silver beads, star sequins, sparkly spaghetti string and glow-in-the-dark fabric paint. You will have fun making and modeling Nighty-nightshirts, comfy Boxer Bottoms and furry Critter Slippers. By sculpting funky Good-dream Fairies out of polymer clay or weaving Dream Catchers from metallic threads, your friends will help bring sweet dreams for all. The jewelry your guests make, such as Shooting-star Earrings and Moonbeam Friendship Bracelets, will shine on long after the last guest leaves your sleepover.

Pajama crafts

Ask each friend to bring a favorite old pair of pajamas to your party. By making them into a pajama bag, a pair of comfy boxer bottoms and two matching bolster pillows, your sleepover pals will make sure these old favorites live happily ever after.

You will need:

★ a pair of old pajamas or a sweat suit (the kind with a pullover top works best)
★ thick yarn
★ polyester fiber stuffing or old, clean panty hose
★ ribbon
★ a measuring tape, straight pins, pinking shears or scissors, a needle and thread

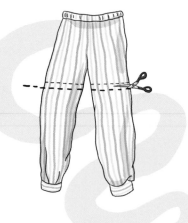

Boxer bottoms

Just add a T-shirt for cool, comfy nightwear.

1. Try on the pajama bottoms and have a friend measure and mark your desired length with straight pins. (Don't go any shorter than 10 cm [4 in.] from the crotch.)

2. Cut off the length below each pin line with pinking shears or scissors, and sew a hem.

Bolster pillows

Use the leftover legs to make two bolster pillows — one for you and one for a friend.

1. Cut off the cuffs with pinking shears.

2. Measure 10 cm (4 in.) up from one end and have a friend gather it in her hand. Wrap 35 cm (14 in.) of coordinating yarn snugly around this gather and tie it in a double-knotted bow. Knot the ends of the yarn so they won't unravel.

3. Stuff from the open end until the pillow is smooth and firm and about 10 cm (4 in.) of fabric is left to gather.

4. Tie off the other end and finish with a double-knotted bow.

Pajama bag

This drawstring bag is made from your pajama top.

1. Cut off both sleeves 2.5 cm (1 in.) from the shoulder seam.

2. Turn the top inside out. Sew the sleeve holes shut with a row of running stitches just outside the shoulder seam.

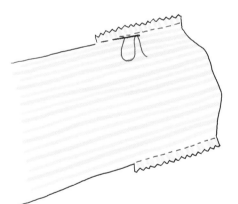

3. Turn the top right side out and then upside down. The waistband becomes the top of your bag and the neckband the bottom.

4. Fold down 1 cm (1/2 in.) of the waistband. Make vertical cuts 0.5 cm (1/4 in.) long on this fold every 2 cm (3/4 in.), all the way round.

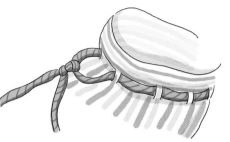

5. Unfold and, starting from the inside, weave two 70 cm (28 in.) lengths of ribbon or yarn (each one knotted at both ends) through the slits.

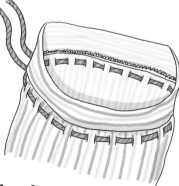

6. Pull the yarn ends up through the slit you began at and knot all ends together.

7. Pull the yarn tight, and the top of your bag is complete.

8. Repeat steps 4 to 7 at the neck to make the bottom of the bag. Tie this end off tightly with double knots so nothing can fall out.

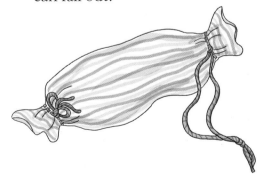

PJ tip

Provide each guest with a plain pillowcase she can decorate with markers. Sign one another's pillows as a keepsake of your party.

Nighty-nightshirt

What could be more comfy for a sleepover than a big T-shirt made special with metallic paints and a few stars? Have your friends bring T-shirts or give them out as a take-home goody.

You will need:

★ a dark-colored, oversize T-shirt (navy, purple or black work well)

★ 12 cm (4½ in.) star nail-heads (optional)

★ metallic or glitter fabric paint and paintbrushes

★ a ruler, scissors or pinking shears, chalk, a thimble, paper or cardboard

1. Fringe the bottom of your T-shirt by cutting up 7.5 cm (3 in.) every 2.5 cm (1 in.).

2. Lightly sketch your design and words (see "Nightshirt expressions" on page 95) with chalk on the front and back. Play around with the stars until you get a pattern you like.

3. If using star nail heads, carefully push the star prongs through the fabric. Turn the shirt inside out and press the prongs down using a thimble. To keep the shirt comfortable for sleeping, use only a few stars and only on the sleeves or hem.

4. Put a piece of paper or cardboard between the shirt layers. On the front, paint your letters, then paint any drawings in your design. Paint a pattern on every other fringe at the front.

5. Let this side of the shirt dry before turning it over to paint the back.

NIGHTSHIRT EXPRESSIONS

* Nighty-night
* Don't let the bedbugs bite
* Sweet dreams
* Who's afraid of the dark?
* Rock around the clock
* Dream on
* Wake me when it's over
* Counting sheep
* I survived Andrea's sleepover

PJ DESIGN POSSIBILITIES

* Brightly colored buttons make funny bedbugs when you glue on roly eyes and paint on legs.
* Heart-shaped buttons around a circular button make great flowers when you paint on stems, leaves or vines.
* Paint a line of flowers, bugs or stars going over the shoulder from front to back.
* If you use a long-sleeved shirt, paint big snoring ZZZZs all the way down one sleeve.

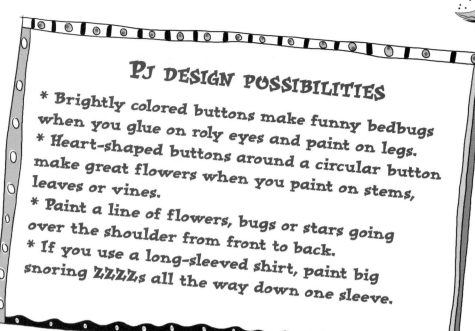

PJ tip

* Work on a hard surface you can lean on and keep a slow, steady hand.
* Paint from the top to the bottom and left to right (right to left if you are left-handed), so you are not dragging your arm through wet paint.
* The thicker your paint, the longer it will take to dry. Metallic paints shine more when dry.
* Wash items decorated with fabric paint in cold water. Hang to dry or tumble dry at a cool setting.

Good-dream fairy

This funky fairy is sure to bring you and your friends sweet dreams. Make a bunch together and send them home the next day to flutter through your friends' rooms.

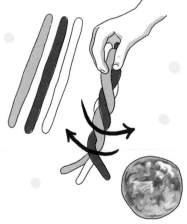

You will need:
★ 3 colors of Fimo or other polymer clay
★ small pearly beads
★ 34 gauge gold wire and a pencil (optional)
★ cardboard
★ gloss clay varnish and a paintbrush (optional)
★ wax paper, toothpicks, plastic knives and forks, a ruler

1. Cover your work surface with wax paper. Have an adult preheat the oven according to the directions on the clay package.

2. Roll a golf ball-sized piece of clay from each color into logs. Cut and set aside a small slice of each for cheeks, hair, a hat, etc.

3. Twist the logs together. Roll this larger log into a marbled ball (just enough to get it smooth but keep the colors separate). Pull off about a quarter of this ball and set it aside for wings.

4. Roll the rest of the ball into a more marbled shade for your fairy's body. Pull off about a quarter of this ball and set it aside for arms.

5. Roll the body ball into a log with a wider head shape lifted up at one end.

6. Use the plastic knife to cut legs into the body. Use your fingers to round the legs and bend the knees back. At the end of each leg, bend the tips into curved fairy boots.

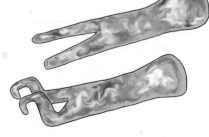

7. Use your fingers to shape the face. Pinch up eyebrows and a nose. Slice the lips open with your knife and press in a mouth. Add cheeks from one of the colors you set aside in step 2. Press a bead into each eye area.

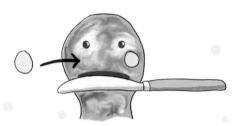

8. Roll out skinny strings of clay from the colors you set aside in step 2, and twist them to look like wavy hair. Cut them to the length you want and attach them to the head.

9. Make three petals from the clay you put aside. Pinch together one end of each petal for a pointy hat. Put the hat on your fairy's head.

10. Roll out arms from the clay you set aside in step 4 and flatten at one end for the hands. Attach the arms by smoothing them onto the shoulders.

11. You will need two hooks to hang your fairy. Make a hook by wrapping a 5 cm (2 in.) piece of wire around a pencil. Twist the ends together and curl each end into a hook. Gently push the hook into your fairy's back and smooth it in. Make another hook the same way.

12. Bake your fairy according to the directions on the clay package. Place small pieces of folded cardboard under the head and feet to keep them from drooping while they bake. Remove from the oven and allow to cool.

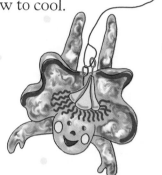

13. Make your fairy shine with a coat of gloss clay varnish, if you like.

SWEET DREAMS

Did you know that ...
* your first dream lasts only a few seconds?
* you have about five dreams in a night?
* all your friends dream, even those who don't remember their dreams?
* some people have dreamed the same dream over and over again for years?
* by the time you are in your 30s, you will have spent five years of your life dreaming?

Dreamy dream catcher

Banish all bad dreams from your sleepover by weaving your own dream catcher. Each sparkly thread you weave will help to filter the good dreams from the bad.

You will need:

★ 2 colors of medium or heavy metallic-braid embroidery floss
★ 30 cm (12 in.) metal hoop
★ pony beads
★ a shaped bead (heart, dog, flower, etc.)
★ colorful feathers
★ a ruler, scissors, glue

1. Tightly tie one end of one color of floss to the hoop, leaving a 20 cm (8 in.) tail.

2. Wrap the floss all the way around the hoop, leaving 1 cm (½ in.) spaces. Tie the floss tightly to the first knot.

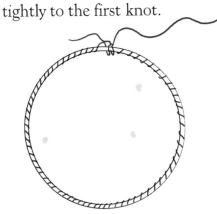

3. Knot one end of the other color of floss to the hoop opposite to where you knotted the first color. Make a loose loop five spaces away. Continue wrapping around the hoop, making a loop every five spaces.

4. Continue looping to make three progressively smaller rows of loops. String on one or two pony beads per row, as you go.

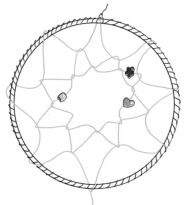

5. When there is a small hole in the center, weave the end of your floss through the last round of loops and pull to tighten.

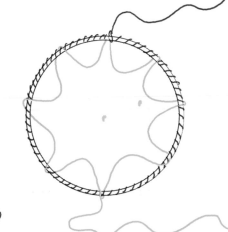

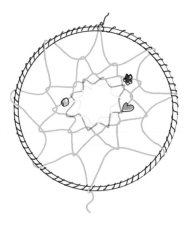

6. To the thread tail, tie a shaped bead symbolic of something that makes you feel safe (a dog, a heart to represent friends, etc.).

7. Cut and tie on two threads about half the length of the bead tail. Tie on a pony bead to each one and then glue a feather hanging down from the beads.

8. Loop two lengths of thread about 15 cm (6 in.) long, around the hoop at the top. Thread a pony bead over the ends. Tie a knot above the pony bead and one 4 cm (1½ in.) from the end. Spread the threads to hang your dream catcher.

DREAM CATCHER SYMBOLISM

* Web — a filter for all dreams (bad dreams are caught and can't pass through)
* Hole — a doorway for the good dreams to pass through
* Feathers at bottom — a way for the good dreams to travel to the dreamer
* Beads — the dream catcher's power will increase through these personal symbols

Critter slippers

Ask each friend to bring a pair of flip-flops or provide them as guest giveaways. Your guests will have fun making and wearing these fuzzy slippers.

You will need:
★ 1 pair of band-style flip-flops
★ fun fur
★ 18 mm roly eyes (2 per slipper)
★ felt scraps
★ a pencil, a ruler, newspaper, straight pins, pinking shears or scissors, thick white glue (tacky)

1. Trace a pattern the same length and 2 cm ($^3/_4$ in.) wider than the width of the flip-flop's band onto the newspaper.

2. Pin the pattern to the fur and cut it out. (If you use pinking shears the material is less likely to fray.)

3. Unpin the pattern. Glue the fur to the band. (some fur may wrap around the band.) Glue on roly eyes.

4. Cut two triangular ears from the felt. To make them stand up, make four 1 cm ($^1/_2$ in.) long cuts evenly spaced on the bottom of each ear. Fold this forward and glue it to the fur.

5. Cut and glue on a triangular felt nose.

6. To make whiskers, cut two 2.5 cm x 4 cm. (1 in. x 1½ in.) fur or felt rectangles. Fringe one edge of each and glue them on either side of the nose.

7. Finish off the mouth by gluing a thin piece of fur to fit around the sole edge.

8. Repeat to make the other slipper.

PJ tip
* You can get great fun-fur bargains by checking the remnants bin at a fabric store. Look for animal prints, pink for pigs, or purple or black for zany wild things.
* Stock up on flip-flops at end-of-summer sales.

Candles

Glow goblet

Make lots of these mini-candleholders and decorate them with fabric paint to match your party theme. They will add a special glow to each guest's place at the table.

You will need:
★ 1 empty 500 mL (16 oz.) plastic bottle with lid
★ fabric paint and a paintbrush
★ a craft knife

1. Have an adult cut the top off the bottle with a craft knife just above the label or where it starts to get round. Set the bottom half aside.

2. Use fabric paint to decorate your goblet on the outside only. Choose a simple design that leaves a lot of unpainted space showing.

3. Set the goblet aside to dry. The thinner the paint, the faster it will dry.

4. To make candles for your Glow Goblet, follow the instructions on page 103, but cut your beeswax into four lengths to make four short candles.

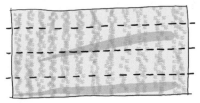

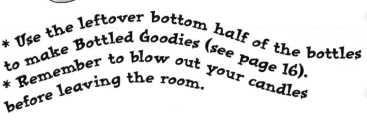

PJ tip
* Use the leftover bottom half of the bottles to make Bottled Goodies (see page 16).
* Remember to blow out your candles before leaving the room.

Beeswax candles

These easy-to-make candles are perfect for a candle holder or for your Glow Goblet.

You will need:

★ 1 sheet of beeswax
★ candlewick
★ scissors, wax paper, a ruler

1. Cut the beeswax in half the long way. Lay one half on a piece of wax paper.

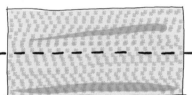

2. Cut a piece of candlewick about 5 cm (2 in.) longer than the width of your beeswax.

3. Lay the wick along the edge of the beeswax with just enough edge left to roll and press over the wick. Roll the wax, keeping the edges even. Press the edge down with your thumb.

4. Trim the wick off one end and leave 1 cm (½ in.) at the other end.

5. Repeat with the other half of the wax sheet.

Star earrings

Shooting-star earrings

Shooting stars, comets, constellations! With a few craft supplies and a little imagination, you and your friends could have the Milky Way dangling from your ears.

You will need:

★ silver metallic thread
★ 1 pair of silver kidney-shaped earring wires
★ 2 small gold beads (4 mm works well)
★ 8 silver star sequins with holes
★ a ruler, scissors

1. Cut two 13 cm (5 in.) pieces of thread. Fold each piece in half.

2. Pull the two threads halfway through the earring wire.

3. Thread all four ends through a gold bead. Knot them snugly under the bead.

4. Separate the threads and thread a sequin onto each. Knot underneath at the desired length — try varying the lengths.

5. Repeat to make the other earring, or use a slightly different pattern.

PJ tip Silver hoops with gold thread and gold stars also look nice.

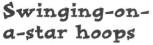

Swinging-on-a-star hoops

How about making some starry hoops that will swing from your ears? Make two and then swap one with a friend for a different look.

You will need:

★ gold or silver elastic cord (for gold hoops, use silver cord and vice versa)
★ a pair of gold or silver hoops (0.25 cm [⅛ in.] or smaller)
★ 4 star-shaped crystal sequins with holes for threading
★ a ruler, scissors, glue

1. Cut two 20 cm (8 in.) lengths of cord.

2. Tie one end of cord just behind the hole of the hoop, leaving enough hoop uncovered to close the earring.

3. Wrap the cord around the hoop, leaving a little space in between.

4. Tie off halfway, at the bottom of the hoop. Cut the cord as close as possible to the knot.

5. Thread two sequins onto the hoop so that they face the front.

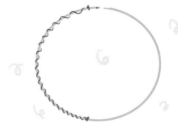

6. Tie and wind the other cord around the rest of the hoop and tie it tightly. Cut the ends close to the knot.

7. To keep the cord from sliding off, dab a drop of glue on each knot.

8. Repeat to make the other earring. Wipe the ends of the earrings with rubbing alcohol before trying them on.

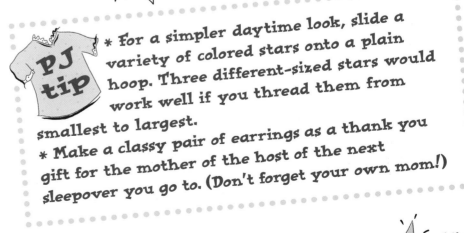

PJ tip

* For a simpler daytime look, slide a variety of colored stars onto a plain hoop. Three different-sized stars would work well if you thread them from smallest to largest.
* Make a classy pair of earrings as a thank you gift for the mother of the host of the next sleepover you go to. (Don't forget your own mom!)

105

Moonbeam jewelry

Moonbeam friendship bracelet

This bracelet is fast and fun to do at a sleepover because you can make it quickly. Gold and silver spaghetti strings spiral together to make a swirl of moonbeams around your wrist.

You will need:

★ gold and silver spaghetti string

★ a measuring stick, scissors, tape

1. Cut a 2.5 m (8 ft.) length of silver spaghetti string. This will be your knotting string (K-string). Cut two 45 cm (18 in.) lengths of gold spaghetti string. These will be your base strings (B-strings).

2. Line up the three strings with your K-string on the left and the two B-strings on the right. Tie these strings into a knot, leaving 8 cm (3 in.) tails. Tape the tails to a table.

3. Wrap the K-string over and under the B-strings and up through its own loop. While holding the B-strings, tug the K-string tightly into a knot.

4. Continue knotting with the K-string five more times. Each knot should appear slightly to the right of the one above it, making a diagonal row.

5. Your K-string should now be at the far right side, almost going underneath the B-strings.

6. Lift your tape and flip your strings over so the K-string is on the left again.

7. Repeat steps 3 to 6, spiraling knots until your bracelet is the length you want.

8. Tie the ends into a knot, leaving 8 cm (3 in.) tails. Snip off any extra length.

Moonbeam ring

Use metallic embroidery floss instead of spaghetti string to make this quick ring.

1. Cut a 75 cm (30 in.) length for the K-string and two 25 cm (10 in.) lengths for the B-strings.

2. Follow steps 2 to 7 for the bracelet.

3. Instead of trimming off the ends, fray them to look like a shower of moonbeams.

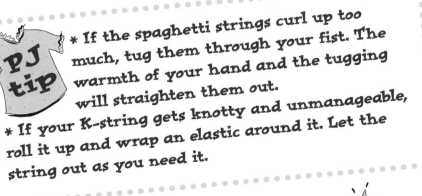

PJ tip
* If the spaghetti strings curl up too much, tug them through your fist. The warmth of your hand and the tugging will straighten them out.
* If your K-string gets knotty and unmanageable, roll it up and wrap an elastic around it. Let the string out as you need it.

Secret anklet

Secrets and sleepovers go together like chips and dip. Pick out alphabet beads to represent your secret: KCB = "Kate has a Crush on Ben" or JJNCST = "Jodie, Julia, Nikki, Claire, Stars of Tomorrow." Then braid your secret into the anklet.

You will need:
★ 2 colors of embroidery floss (1 plain, 1 metallic)
★ alphabet beads with holes big enough to pull two strands of floss through
★ a ruler, scissors, tape

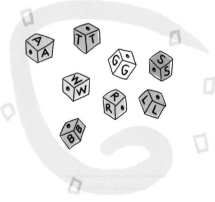

1. Cut two 30 cm (12 in.) lengths of the plain floss and one of the metallic.

2. Knot the pieces together 5 cm (2 in.) from the end and tape that end to a table.

3. Braid down about 5 cm (2 in.) and thread the two plain threads through your first bead.

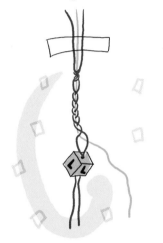

4. Braid 2.5 cm (1 in.) more and thread the next bead onto the two plain threads. Repeat braiding and beading until all the beads are woven into the threads.

5. Hold the anklet around your ankle, and see how much more you need to braid. Finish braiding, leaving enough thread to tie a knot.

PJ tip

* When threading on the alphabet beads, make sure they will read in the correct order once on your ankle.
* If your secret requires more than five or six beads, make a necklace instead by doubling the length of the floss to 50 cm (20 in.).
* Make a Secret Anklet for each guest ahead of time. Then see if your guests can guess the secret.

Nighttime necklaces

Circle-of-friends necklace

This choker-style necklace is a cooperative effort that will represent the unity and individuality of your circle of friends when it is complete.

You will need:

★ small and large clear, colored beads

★ memory wire long enough to circle a neck, with a little extra to turn back at each end

★ pliers

1. Each friend chooses a different color of bead and counts out eight beads for each of her friends and for herself.

2. Decide on one different color of bead to represent your group. Give each guest the same number of these as there are friends at the party.

3. Each friend chooses a unique larger bead. Design your bead pattern around this large bead. Will you keep each friend's beads separate? Will you make a sequenced pattern or a jumble of beads? How will you use the group beads?

4. Use the pliers to bend back one end of the memory wire so the beads won't fall off.

5. String your beads onto the other end in the pattern you have chosen. Bend this end back, put on your necklace and be circled in your friendships wherever you go.

PJ tip This necklace makes a great keepsake gift for a friend who has to move away.

110

Lady-in-the-moon pendant

You and your guests will moon over one another's glimmering necklaces.

You will need:
★ Fimo or other polymer clay
★ 2 small round beads
★ glitter fabric paint and a brush
★ metallic braid floss
★ a ruler, scissors, a plastic knife or toothpick, a pen

1. Flatten a clay ball the size of a large gumball into a disc about twice as thick as a coin.

2. Pinch up a bit of clay at the center for a nose. Pinch up cheekbones and eyebrows. Press two beads into the eye hollows and remove, leaving eye holes.

3. Use the tip of a plastic knife or a toothpick to make a smiling mouth and lips.

4. Use a pen to make a hole for the cord near the top.

5. Have an adult help you bake the pendant according to the directions on the clay package. Remove from the oven and allow to cool.

6. To make your pendant sparkly, put a few small drops of glitter fabric paint on the face and rub a thin layer over the surface with your finger.

7. Cut two 80 cm (32 in.) pieces of metallic braid or ribbon. Fold the two pieces in half and thread the fold from back to front through the hole. Now thread the other ends through this loop and snugly pull through.

8. Tie the ends into a double knot so you can put the necklace over your head without undoing it.

Treasure boxes

Bedtime boxes

Need a box for your hair scrunchees, retainer, party photos or secret notes? With Shooting-star Earrings (page 104) tucked inside, these glitzy boxes make great guest goodies.

You will need:

★ 1 star-shaped box (available at craft supply stores)
★ 3 colors of paint and paintbrushes
★ old magazines
★ a sealer product such as Podgy or Mod Podge and a small paintbrush
★ scissors

1. Paint the top and edges of the box lid one color and leave it to dry.

2. Paint the points on the box bottom alternating colors and leave to dry.

3. Cut out pictures of your favorite stars and heroes from magazines. Arrange and overlap the photos in different ways until you get a collage you like.

4. When the lid is dry, place your collage on top and carefully brush the Podgy over the pictures and the entire surface of the lid. Leave it to dry. Apply one more coat of Podgy and leave it to dry.

5. Paint the box bottom while the top is drying.

Shine on paint-and-sticker box

You will need:
★ 1 moon-shaped box
★ 2 colors of metallic paint (bronze and silver look great together) and paintbrushes
★ star and moon stickers
★ fabric paint and a paintbrush
★ gloss Podgy and a paintbrush (optional)

1. Paint the top of the lid with one color. Paint the sides of the lid with the other color. Leave to dry.

2. When the lid is dry, put the stickers on.

3. Add dimension to the stickers by thinly outlining them with a contrasting fabric paint. Leave to dry.

4. Seal the surface of your box and lid with two layers of Podgy if you like, letting the first layer dry before adding the next.

Glitzy boxes

You will need:
★ small wooden stars (two sizes)
★ metallic and/or glittery fabric paint
★ 1 small cardboard jewelry box
★ a glue gun or craft glue

1. Paint the wooden stars by squirting a drop of fabric paint onto each one and smoothing it on with your finger. Leave to dry.

2. Glue the stars to the lid in the design you want, covering the store label if there is one.

PJ tip
* A shoe box, candy box or any box with a lid can be painted and decorated to make a variation on the boxes above.
* Make a stack of coordinated boxes, from large to small, to store your hair accessories, nail polish and jewelry.
* Instead of using metallic fabric paint, try neon or glow-in-the-dark.

COOKING UP A SLEEPOVER

WHAT COULD BE MORE FUN THAN all your buddies in your kitchen cooking up sensational sleepover meals and snacks? You may want to prepare some meals in advance or make them assembly-line style with your friends during the party. Make sure everyone can enjoy the food by asking ahead of time about any special food needs or allergies.

Snoop through the recipes to find ones that match your party theme. You and your fellow night owls won't mind getting up in the morning when it's for a Yogurt Sundae Bar Buffet or a yummy Bananarama Wrap. So gather your friends and your ingredients and cook up a delicious sleepover. Remember to check with your parents for permission or help when using the stove or microwave. Use a pair of oven mitts to handle hot saucepans, baking sheets or cake pans.

MEASURING INGREDIENTS

Both metric and imperial systems of measurement are used in this book. The systems vary a little, so choose one and use it for all your measuring. Here are the abbreviations used in the recipes:

METRIC:
mL = milliliter
L = liter
g = gram
kg = kilogram
pkg. = package

IMPERIAL:
tsp. = teaspoon
tbsp. = tablespoon
oz. = ounce
lb. = pound
c. = cup

D·I·N·N·E·R·S
Mainly Mexican

Senorita nachos

Your friends will shout "Olé!" when you serve these.

You will need:

250 g	medium ground beef (optional)	½ lb.
250 mL	diced tomato	1 c.
250 mL	diced sweet red pepper	1 c.
125 mL	diced onion (optional)	½ c.
125 mL	sliced olives (optional)	½ c.
500 mL	grated cheddar cheese	2 c.
500 mL	grated mozzarella cheese	2 c.
1	large bag of white corn tortilla chips	1

frying pan ★ a sharp knife
measuring cups
a mixing bowl ★ a spoon
2 baking sheets or pizza pans

1. If you're using meat, fry the ground beef until it is brown and crumbly and all the pink is gone. Drain well. Set aside.

2. Mix the tomato and sweet pepper together in a bowl.

3. Layer half the chips, all the meat and half the sweet pepper and tomatoes on one baking sheet. Make the other sheet without meat.

4. Before adding onions and olives, ask your guests' preferences and add to the trays accordingly. Top with both cheeses.

5. Broil one sheet at a time for a few minutes or until the cheese starts to bubble.

Serves 4 to 6

MEXICAN MEAL SUGGESTIONS

Beverages — limeade in tall, iced glasses, garnished with lemon and lime slices

Veggies — carrot, celery and zucchini sticks with guacamole

Dessert — a "cactus" per guest, made by piling two scoops of lime green sherbet in a dessert dish and decorating with green gumdrops for thorns

116

Thick and chunky nacho dip

Invite your guests to dip nachos or plain tortilla chips into this yummy dip. Mix the following ingredients together for a medium-hot dip.

You will need:

369 mL	can tomato paste	13 fl. oz.
125 mL	chunky salsa	½ c.
75 mL	mustard	⅓ c.
2 mL	crushed red pepper	½ tsp.
2 mL	garlic powder	½ tsp.
2 mL	Tabasco sauce	½ tsp.
15 mL	brown sugar	1 tbsp.

SOME LIKE IT HOT

You can adjust the dip's seasoning to suit your guests' tastes.

Mild — Leave out the red pepper and Tabasco sauce.

Hot cha cha — Double the amount of red pepper and Tabasco.

Tongue burner — Make Hot cha cha and then add 75 mL (⅓ c.) chopped pickled jalapeño peppers.

PJ POSSIBILITY

If your guests all like different toppings, put the toppings in separate containers on a serving tray. Broil the nachos with just the cheese on, and let everyone add her own combination of toppings. Include a dish of pickled jalapeños for those who dare and some sour cream to soothe fiery taste buds.

Not just a sandwich

Sloppy josies

These sweet and sloppy sandwiches are easy to make and fun to eat.

You will need:

500 g	medium ground beef	1 lb.
1 mL	onion powder	¼ tsp.
125 mL	ketchup	½ c.
50 mL	mustard	¼ c.
15 mL	sugar	1 tbsp.
	or	
2	packets artificial sweetener	2
15 mL	pickle vinegar	1 tbsp.
	(straight from the pickle jar)	
3 drops	Tabasco sauce	3 drops
6	hamburger buns	6

measuring cups and spoons
a frying pan with a lid
a bowl ★ a large fork ★ a strainer

1. Break up the ground beef while putting it into the frying pan. Fry the beef until it is brown and crumbly and all the pink is gone. Sprinkle onion powder over the meat and stir it in.

2. While the meat is browning, stir together the ketchup, mustard, sweetener, pickle vinegar and Tabasco sauce.

3. Use the strainer to drain all grease off the meat. Return the meat to the pan.

4. Pour the sauce over the browned meat and stir with a fork until well coated. Cover and cook for 5 minutes on low, stirring halfway through.

5. To steam the buns, lay the bottom halves face down on the meat mixture. Place the tops on top. Cover and steam on low until the buns are soft and warm.

6. Remove the buns and spread the mixture over the bottoms. Cover with the tops and serve hot.

Serves 6

B.A.C.O.M. baguettes

B.A.C.O.M. is an acronym for the ingredients (bacon, almonds, cheese, onion, mayonnaise) of these mini open-face sandwiches.

You will need:

1	baguette (long, skinny french bread)	1
6 slices	bacon	6 slices
75 g	slivered almonds (optional)	4 oz.
125 mL	grated cheese	½ c.
125 mL	diced onion	½ c.
125 mL	mayonnaise	½ c.

measuring cups ★ a sharp knife
a grater ★ a bread knife
a baking sheet ★ a frying pan
paper towels
a medium mixing bowl ★ a spoon

1. Cut the baguette into slices about 2 cm (³/₄ in.) thick. Arrange on the baking sheet. Set aside.

2. Fry the bacon until crispy. Remove it from the pan and lay on paper towel to drain. Pat gently with another sheet of paper towel to remove the grease. When it is cool, crumble the bacon into small bits.

3. In the bowl, mix together the bacon, cheese, mayonnaise, onion and almonds, if using.

4. Spread the mixture on the bread slices.

5. Bake at 200°C (400°F) for about 12 minutes. Serve warm.

Makes 20 to 24 slices

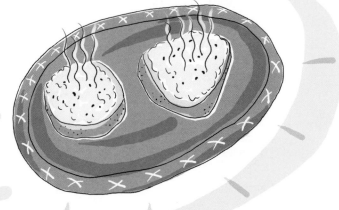

PJ tip
* Use cocktail rye bread (comes in mini-slices) instead of a sliced baguette.
* Serve these for breakfast instead of lunch or dinner.

Party pasta

Chili fusilli

This pasta is as much fun to make as it is to say.

You will need:

1.5 L	fusilli pasta	6 c.
	(or radiatore or rotini)	
375 mL	canned black beans	1½ c.
500 mL	chili sauce	2 c.
500 mL	grated Monterey Jack cheese	2 c.

measuring cups ★ a grater
a large pot ★ a microwavable container
a spoon

1. Cook the fusilli according to the directions on the package.

2. Pour the drained beans into the microwavable container. Add chili sauce and stir.

3. Heat on high in the microwave for 2 minutes.

4. Pour the chili-bean sauce over the pasta and toss well.

5. Sprinkle 125 mL (½ c.) of cheese on each serving.

Serves 4 to 6

Heavenly angel-hair pasta

These little pasta nests look and taste gourmet, but they are quick and easy to make.

You will need:

4 nests	angel-hair pasta	4 nests
150 mL	olive oil	²/₃ c.
325 mL	grated Parmesan cheese	1¹/₃ c.
	grated peel of 1 lemon	
5 mL	lemon pepper or black pepper	1 tsp.
	pine nuts or parsley flakes (optional)	

measuring cups and spoons
a grater ★ a large pot
a small microwavable container ★ a spoon

1. Cook the fragile angel-hair pasta with care according to the directions on the package.

2. Pour the olive oil into the microwavable container. Add Parmesan cheese and the grated lemon peel and stir well.

3. Cook on high for 40 seconds. Stir well.

4. Pour immediately into the center of the cooked pasta nests. Sprinkle each serving with 1 mL (¹/₄ tsp.) of pepper. Add pine nuts or parsley flakes, if using.

Serves 4

Oriental linguine

Try eating this East-meets-Italy dish with chopsticks.

You will need:

1 handful	per person of linguine (or spaghettini)	1 handful
	vegetable oil	
375 g box	Oriental-style frozen stir-fry vegetables	13 oz.
250 mL	honey dijon salad dressing	1 c.
125 mL	cashews (optional)	¹/₂ c.

measuring cups ★ a large pot
a frying pan ★ a spatula
a mixing spoon

1. Cook the linguine according to the directions on the package.

2. Heat the vegetable oil in the frying pan until hot and add the frozen vegetables. Use the spatula to stir over high heat for 3 to 4 minutes or until the vegetables are cooked through but still crunchy.

3. Pour the dressing onto the cooked pasta. Stir until all pasta is coated.

4. Add the vegetables to the pasta. Stir well.

5. Sprinkle cashews on each serving, if you like.

Serves 4 to 6

Pita pizza pizzazz

Smokin' pita pizza

You can easily make delicious pizzas by using pitas as a base.

You will need:

1	pita	1
25 mL	smoky barbecue sauce	2 tbsp.
3	marinated sun-dried tomatoes or	3
50 mL	chopped sweet red pepper	¼ c.
½ slice	smoked chicken or ham (optional)	½ slice
75 mL	grated Asiago cheese or other smoked cheese	⅓ c.

measuring cups and spoons
a sharp knife ★ a grater
a baking sheet ★ a large spoon

1. Place the pita with the flattest side down on the baking sheet. Spread barbecue sauce over the pita.

2. Arrange the sundried tomatoes or sweet peppers on the pita.

3. Tuck the smoked chicken slice between the sundried tomatoes.

4. Sprinkle cheese evenly over the pizza.

5. Broil for a few minutes or until the cheese melts.

6. Cut into four slices and serve.

Makes 1 personal pizza

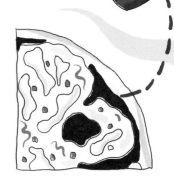

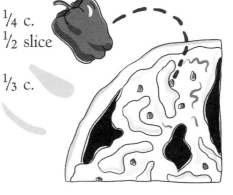

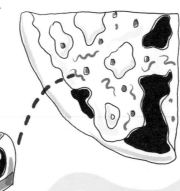

Greek pita pizza

You will need:

1	pita	1
15 mL	Greek salad dressing	1 tbsp.
75 mL	finely chopped tomatoes	1/3 c.
50 mL	sliced black olives	1/4 c.
75 mL	crumbled feta cheese	1/3 c.

measuring cups and spoons
a sharp knife ★ a baking sheet
a spoon ★ paper towel

1. Place the pita with the flattest side down on the baking sheet. Spread salad dressing over the pita.

2. Remove excess liquid from the tomatoes by laying them on paper towel and patting. Arrange them on the pita.

3. Add the olives and sprinkle on feta cheese.

4. Broil for 1 to 2 minutes or until the cheese starts to turn a light golden brown.

5. Cut into four slices and serve.

Makes 1 pizza

Baby three-cheese pizzas

You will need:

12	baby pitas	12
50 mL	prepared tomato or pasta sauce	1/4 c.
175 mL	each of cheese — mozzarella, cheddar and Parmesan	3/4 c.

measuring cups and spoons
a grater ★ a baking sheet
a bowl ★ a spoon

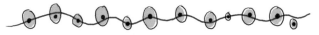

1. Arrange the pitas on the baking sheet. Spread 5 mL (1 tsp.) of sauce over each pita.

2. Pour grated cheeses into a bowl and mix. Sprinkle 15 mL (1 tbsp.) of cheese over each pita.

3. Broil for a few minutes or until the cheese begins to bubble.

Serves 4 (makes 12 baby pizzas)

These take the cake

Toffee-bar-topping cake

Icing a cake is the best part — and that's all you need to do when you start with a pre-made cake.

You will need:

1	angel food cake	1
4	chocolate-covered toffee bars	4
500 mL	whipping cream	2 c.
125 mL	icing sugar	½ c.

measuring cups ★ a medium mixing bowl
a long-bladed knife ★ an electric mixer
a rolling pin ★ a spatula ★ a cake plate

1. Chill the chocolate toffee bars and mixing bowl in the refrigerator.

2. Cut the cake in half horizontally. Lay the top half upside down on the counter. Place the bottom half on the cake plate.

3. Pour the whipping cream into the bowl. Beat on high about 3 minutes or until stiff.

4. Leaving the chocolate bars in their wrappers, roll a rolling pin back and forth over each bar until it is in small bits.

5. Remove the wrappers over the whipping cream bowl and drop in the bits. Fold in gently with the spatula.

6. Spread some topping over the bottom half of the cake with the spatula.

7. Gently place the top half on top. Spread topping over the top and sides of the cake.

8. Refrigerate until ready to serve.

Chocolate strawberry pizza-cakes

Some of your pals may eat pizza for breakfast, but this decadent one is definitely for dessert.

You will need:

1	brownie mix	1
75 mL	vegetable oil	⅓ c.
2	eggs	2
1	container of chocolate icing	1
250 mL	hulled and quartered strawberries	1 c.
3	squares white chocolate	3

measuring cups ★ a sharp knife
2 round, greased pizza pans
a large mixing bowl ★ a large spoon
a table knife

1. Preheat the oven to 350°F (180°C).

2. Combine the brownie mix, oil, eggs and water in the mixing bowl. Blend with the large spoon until the mixture is wet and smooth.

3. Pour half the mixture onto each pizza pan. Smooth the tops with the back of the spoon if necessary.

4. Place the pans on separate racks. Bake for 12 to 15 minutes. Halfway through, switch the pans onto the other racks.

5. The pizzas are done when a toothpick inserted into the center comes out clean.

6. Let cool before icing. Drop spoonfuls of icing on and smooth with the spoon. Use a table knife to draw lines for eight equal pizza pieces.

7. Decorate with the strawberries.

8. Melt the white chocolate squares in the microwave on high for 1½ minutes and then stir. Drizzle this white chocolate "cheese" onto the pizzas.

D·E·S·S·E·R·T·S
Light and delicious desserts

Starry night Jell-O

Can you imagine eating a bowlful of midnight blue sky covered with stars?

You will need:

1	package Berry Blue or Berry Black Jell-O or other blue-colored gelatin mix	1
1	envelope clear unflavored gelatin	1
1	package of Sparkling White Grape or yellow Jell-O or other light-colored gelatin mix	1
300 mL	ginger ale	1¼ c.

measuring cups ★ 4 dessert cups
a mixing bowl ★ a spoon
a greased rectangular pan
a medium-sized star-shaped cookie cutter

1. Make the blue Jell-O according to the directions on the package. Pour equal amounts into the four dessert cups and put in the refrigerator to set.

2. Pour the clear gelatin into 175 mL (³/₄ c.) of boiling water. Add sparkling Jell-O powder and stir until all gelatin and Jell-O crystals are completely dissolved (at least 2 minutes).

3. Stir in the ginger ale.

4. Pour the mixture into the greased pan so that it is no deeper than the thickness of the cookie cutter. Chill for 4 hours or until firm.

5. Use the cookie cutter to carefully press out sparkly Jell-O stars.

6. Place two stars on each cup of Jell-O.

Serves 4

Marshmallow pudding puffs

What could be yummier than these bite-sized puff pastries filled with pudding and marshmallows?

You will need:

1	package of cooked pudding and pie filling (not instant)	1
375 mL	miniature marshmallows	1½ c.
24	mini puff-pastry shells (or 12 regular size)	24

measuring cups ★ a medium pot
a mixing spoon

1. Prepare the pudding mix according to the directions on the package.

2. Remove from stove and let cool for 5 minutes.

3. Blend in 250 mL (1 c.) of the marshmallows until completely melted and mixed into the pudding.

4. Carefully spoon pudding into the shells before it sets.

5. Top each pudding puff with a miniature marshmallow.

Makes 24 mini puffs or 12 regular puffs

PJ tip You will have enough pudding left over to make four servings of rocky road pudding. Alternate layers of miniature marshmallows and pudding in dessert cups. Chill and serve.

Drop-dead cookies

Butterscotch clouds

These heavenly marshmallow cookies taste like biting into coconutty butterscotch clouds.

You will need:

125 g	cream cheese	4 oz.
25 mL	milk	2 tbsp.
500 mL	icing sugar	2 c.
250 mL	butterscotch chips	1 c.
750 mL	miniature marshmallows	3 c.
200 g	flaked coconut	7 oz.

measuring cups and spoons
a table knife ★ a large mixing bowl
an electric mixer ★ a microwavable container
a spoon ★ a small flat-bottomed bowl
2 baking sheets lined with wax paper

1. Cut the cream cheese into quarters and place in the mixing bowl.

2. Add the milk and beat until smooth.

3. Add half the icing sugar and mix on low speed until blended. Add the rest and mix again.

4. Pour the butterscotch chips into the microwavable container. Cook in the microwave on high for 1 minute, stir and then heat for 1 minute and stir again. Add to the mixing bowl and blend well.

5. Add the marshmallows and stir well by hand until all are coated with the butterscotch mixture.

6. Spread a layer of coconut in the flat-bottomed bowl. Drop a spoonful of the butterscotch mixture in the coconut and roll until coated. Set on a baking sheet.

7. Chill the cookies until firm and not sticky. Store in the refrigerator until you are ready to eat them.

Makes approximately 40 cookies

Smart flakes

You will have fun stirring up and gobbling down these chewy cookies.

You will need:

125 mL	brown sugar	½ c.
125 mL	corn syrup	½ c.
125 mL	peanut butter	½ c.
750 mL	corn flakes or other cereal flakes	3 c.
125 mL	Smarties or M&Ms or other candy-coated chocolate	½ c.

measuring cups
a medium saucepan ★ a spoon
a baking sheet lined with wax paper

1. Mix the brown sugar, corn syrup and peanut butter in the saucepan.

2. Bring to a boil over medium-high heat. Stir constantly for 1 minute to keep from sticking or scorching. Remove from heat.

3. Gently stir in cereal until well coated. Add M&Ms and stir gently.

4. Drop by spoonfuls onto the baking sheet.

5. Store in the refrigerator until you are ready to eat them.

Makes approximately 24 small cookies

Cook up some candy

Cookies-and-cream bark

You may want to make two batches of this because everyone will be barking for more.

You will need:

6	squares white chocolate	6
6	chocolate-sandwich cookies	6

a pizza pan lined with wax paper
a knife ★ a microwavable bowl ★ a spoon

1. Use your hands to break the cookies into bits. Spread them evenly over the pizza pan, but not too close to the edges.

2. Cut the chocolate squares in half and put them in the microwavable bowl. Microwave on high for 2 minutes and stir. If they aren't totally melted, cook 1 minute more and stir until smooth.

3. Pour melted chocolate over the cookie bits until all are covered.

4. Place in the refrigerator for about 1 hour. Lift the bark off the wax paper and break into pieces.

PJ tip To make almond bark, substitute toasted almonds for the cookie bits.

Choco-cherry fudge stars

These fudgy stars will disappear like the night.

You will need:

700 g	semisweet chocolate chips	1¼ c.
300 mL	sweetened condensed milk	1 can
50 mL	maraschino cherry juice	¼ c.

measuring cups
a microwavable bowl ★ a spoon
a baking sheet lined with wax paper
(including the sides)
a medium-sized star-shaped cookie cutter

1. Stir the chocolate chips and condensed milk in the microwavable bowl until milk coats all the chips.

2. Cook on high in the microwave for 1½ minutes. Stir and then cook another 1½ minutes.

3. Add the cherry juice and stir until all chocolate is melted and smooth.

4. Spread the choco-cherry mixture on the cookie sheet so that it is slightly thinner than the thickness of the cookie cutter. Smooth the top with the back of the spoon.

5. Place in the refrigerator for about 1 hour.

6. Turn the baking sheet over onto a cutting surface and peel off the wax paper.

7. Use the cookie cutter to cut out star shapes. Store in the refrigerator.

PJ tip

* If you are going to make fudge stars during your party, gather up more than one cookie cutter. Cut the slab in half, so that more guests can press out stars at one time.
* Try using white chocolate chips to make half of your fudge, so that you have light and dark stars.
* Shake candy sprinkles over the fudge before you refrigerate it.

Bagel chips

Don't throw out those stale bagels. You can cut and cook them into delicious dippers.

You will need:

4	stale bagels (you can buy day-old bagels inexpensively)	4
25 mL	light cooking oil	2 tbsp.
	seasonings (such as garlic, cinnamon, grated Parmesan, chili powder)	

measuring spoons ★ a bread knife
2 baking sheets ★ a basting brush

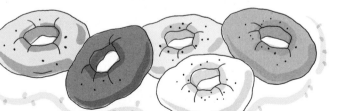

1. Preheat oven to 350°F (180°C).

2. Cut bagels in half vertically. Slice each half into three, and halve each slice. Place them cut-side up on a baking sheet.

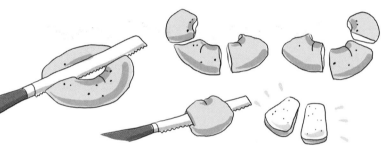

3. Lightly brush the bagel pieces with oil.

4. Sprinkle on seasoning to taste. Try blending some seasonings, such as chili powder and Parmesan.

5. Bake for 10 minutes. Leave out to cool and crisp.

PJ tip These can be baked ahead of time and stored in an airtight container.

Dips

Basic dip

You can make different dips for veggies, fruit or bagel chips just by stirring in different ingredients. Mix the following two ingredients together, then add one or more dippy stir-ins.

You will need:

250 mL	well-drained low-fat cottage cheese	1 c.
125 mL	low-fat sour cream	½ c.

Dippy stir-ins

50 mL	chunky salsa	¼ c.
50 mL	red pepper jelly	¼ c.
50 mL	shrimp cocktail sauce	¼ c.
15 mL	curry powder	1 tbsp.
25 mL	peach chutney	2 tbsp
100 mL	drained pineapple bits	½ c.
25 mL	slivered almonds, toasted	2 tbsp.
25 mL	sweetened feather-strip coconut, toasted	2 tbsp.
⅓ pkg.	dried soup mix (onion or vegetable)	⅓ pkg.

PJ tip

* Spicy dips, such as salsa or onion, work well with vegetables and chips.
* Sweet dips made with chutney or coconut are good with fruits, such as apples or grapes.
* Serve dips in hollowed-out fruits or vegetables, such as melons, pineapples or red peppers.
* Dips made with sour cream or cottage cheese should be refrigerated until serving.

Personalized popcorn

YOUR KITCHEN WILL BE POPPING with wild and spicy recipes when you invite your friends to shake up their own flavored popcorn. Set out some seasonings and give each friend a blank recipe card and a large plastic sandwich bag filled with about 500 mL (2 c.) of popcorn. Ask her to try one of the seasoning suggestions here or concoct her own recipes, name it and record the ingredients.

Pickled cowpoke
1 mL	ranch dressing	¼ tsp.
1 mL	dill weed	¼ tsp.

Nacho
1 mL	ground chili powder	¼ tsp.
1 mL	paprika	¼ tsp.
1 mL	ground cumin	¼ tsp.
15 mL	Monterey Jack cheese	1 tbsp.

Apple cinnamon
1 mL	cinnamon	¼ tsp.
1 mL	brown sugar	¼ tsp.
50 mL	dried apple chips	¼ c.

Spicy monkey
1 mL	soya sauce	¼ tsp.
1 mL	garlic powder	¼ tsp.
0.5 mL	cayenne pepper	⅛ tsp.
50 mL	dried banana chips	¼ c.

Double lemon
1 mL	lemon pepper	¼ tsp.
5 mL	shredded lemon peel	1 tsp.

Easy cheezy
15 mL	grated Parmesan cheese	1 tbsp.
	or	
15 mL	finely shredded cheddar	1 tbsp.

HOW DOES POPCORN POP?

Every kernel of popcorn has a small drop of water stored inside a soft pocket of starch, which is protected by the kernel's hard shell. As the kernel heats up, the water starts to expand and pressure from the steam builds against the starch. The starch inflates, bursts and turns the kernel inside out while releasing the water's steam.

POPCORN POSSIBILITIES

Experiment with a sprinkle of some of these spices and seasonings. Remember, a little goes a long way.

* dill weed, paprika, onion powder, garlic powder, cayenne pepper, lemon pepper, curry powder, oregano

Mixed-up munchies

Fish'n rods

Mix and bake your favorite munchies for a midnight snack taste sensation.

You will need:

125 mL	butter	½ c.
125 mL	light cooking oil	½ c.
5 mL	garlic powder	1 tsp.
2 mL	onion powder	½ tsp.
5 mL	salt	1 tsp.
25 mL	Worcestershire sauce	2 tbsp.
5 mL	curry powder	1 tsp.
500 mL	fish-shaped crackers	2 c.
500 mL	Cheerios or other toasted oat cereal	2 c.
500 mL	pretzel sticks	2 c.
250 mL	hickory sticks	1 c.
250 mL	Cheezies or other crispy cheese twists	1 c.

measuring cups and spoons
a medium roasting pan ★ a mixing spoon

1. Preheat oven to 300°F (150°C).

2. Stir butter, oil and seasonings in the roasting pan over medium heat until melted.

3. Add all other ingredients in order. Stir until coated with the butter and oil mixture.

4. Bake for 45 minutes or until crispy, stirring from top to bottom every 15 minutes.

5. Let cool and store in the cereal and cracker boxes or airtight containers.

PJ tip

You can mix and match different cereals and crackers with your favorite snack foods. Just make sure that your total amount of crackers, cereals and snack foods adds up to 2 L (8 c.).

Cereals — crispy, bite-sized, unsweetened cereals

Crackers — miniature crackers that won't get soggy when baked

Snacks — almost anything salty (this is a great way to use up leftovers)

Rain forest trail mix

This mixture will take you on a tropical taste adventure.

You will need:

500 mL	sunflower seeds	2 c.
125 mL	slivered almonds	½ c.
125 mL	shredded coconut	½ c.
25 mL	butter	2 tbsp.
10 mL	salt	2 tsp.
250 mL	dried pineapple bits, halved	1 c.
250 mL	dried apricots, quartered	1 c.
125 mL	raisins	½ c.

measuring cups and spoons
a medium mixing bowl ★ a mixing spoon
a baking sheet ★ a sharp knife

1. Preheat oven to 300°F (150°C).

2. Pour sunflower seeds, almonds and coconut into the mixing bowl.

3. Melt the butter and add salt. Pour this over the sunflower seed mixture. Stir until well coated.

4. Spread in a thin layer on the baking sheet. Bake about 20 minutes or until lightly toasted. Turn after 5 minutes.

5. Put the pineapple and apricots into the bowl. Add the raisins and the sunflower seed mixture. Mix well.

6. Store in an airtight container.

PJ tip This makes a high-energy camp snack for your campers at Camp N.B.A. (page 30) — prepackage it in individual plastic bags.

Fruity and fun

Yogurt sundae bar buffet

How would you like to serve your guests sundaes for breakfasts? Organize the yogurt toppings before the party.

You will need:

★ a variety of yogurt flavors (estimate a little more than 250 mL (1 c.) per guest)
★ fresh or canned fruit: strawberries, kiwifruit, blueberries, raspberries, melon, fruit cocktail, mandarin oranges, pineapple, apricots, peaches
★ toppings: jam, honey, corn syrup, maple syrup
★ sprinkles: granola, sesame seeds, sunflower seeds, coconut, raisins

a sharp knife
1 serving dish per ingredient
plastic wrap ★ spoons
dessert dishes

1. Wash and cut fruit into bite-size portions. Put each type of fruit in a serving dish, cover with plastic wrap and chill. If using canned fruit, partially drain off the liquid.

2. Pour each topping into a separate dish.

3. Put the sprinkles in small dishes.

4. Arrange all ingredients on a counter or table where guests can serve themselves.

Fruit kebabs

Make up little fruit kebabs by sliding a maraschino cherry, pineapple chunk and strawberry slice onto a cocktail toothpick. Include them as a fancy garnish to the yogurt sundaes.

Strawberry monkey smoothie

Serve your guests this pretty pink smoothie in tall glasses. It is a nutritious, delicious breakfast from a blender. For a strawberry monkey milkshake, add 125 mL ($\frac{1}{2}$ c.) of milk.

You will need:

$\frac{1}{2}$	chopped banana	$\frac{1}{2}$
3	large strawberries, sliced	3
3	heaping scoops of vanilla ice cream or frozen yogurt	3

a sharp knife ★ a blender
1 tall glass per person

1. Put all ingredients into the blender.

2. Blend on high for 10 to 15 seconds.

3. Pour into a tall glass.

Mock champagne

Make this sparkling punch just before serving so it will keep its bubbly fizz.

You will need:

	seedless grapes	
1 L	white grape juice	4 c.
1 L	lemon or lime sparkling water	4 c.

measuring cups ★ an ice-cube tray
a punch bowl or juice pitcher
punch cups or stemmed glasses

1. Place two grapes in each section of an empty ice-cube tray. Freeze for 2 hours.

2. Pour the white grape juice into the punch bowl or pitcher.

3. Slowly add the sparkling water and frozen grapes. Serve in punch cups or stemmed glasses.

Wrap and roll

YOU CAN USE DIFFERENT KINDS OF INTERNATIONAL FLATBREADS, such as tortillas, pitas, roti, rice paper or chapati, as wrappers. Keep your wrappers stacked and covered until you need each one, to prevent drying.

Wrap it up

1. Lay your wrapper on a clean, dry, flat surface. Place the filling down the center, with slightly more in the middle than at the ends.

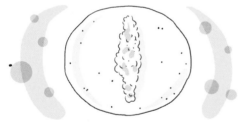

2. Fold the wrapper up about 2.5 cm (1 in.) from the bottom. Squeeze gently along the fold line with your thumb and index finger. Hold the fold in place with your left hand while folding the right side over the filling with your right hand.

3. Fold the left side of the wrapper over the right so the filling is surrounded, except at the top.

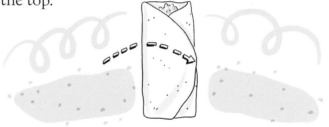

4. Wrap the bottom third of the wrap in a paper napkin. It will make this handheld breakfast easier for your sleepy friends to handle.

Breakfast berry wrap

You will need:

1	whole wheat tortilla or other wrapper	1
125 mL	cottage cheese	½ c.
10 mL	strawberry jam or other flavor	2 tsp.
50 mL	sliced strawberries or other berries	¼ c.

measuring cups and spoons
a sharp knife ★ a spoon

1. Spoon the cottage cheese in a line across the center of the tortilla.

2. Drizzle the jam over the cottage cheese.

3. Layer the sliced strawberries on top.

4. Roll up your wrap.

Makes 1 wrap

B.L.T. wrap

You will need:

1	corn tortilla or other wrapper mayonnaise	1
1 or 2	lettuce leaves	1 or 2
½	medium-sized tomato, diced	½
1 strip	fried, drained and crumbled bacon ketchup	1 strip

a sharp knife ★ a knife ★ a spoon

1. Spread the tortilla with a thin layer of mayonnaise.

2. Cover all but the outside edges of the tortilla with lettuce.

3. Lay the diced tomato in a vertical line down the center of the tortilla.

4. Sprinkle the bacon bits on top.

5. Add ketchup to taste and roll up your wrap.

Makes 1 wrap

Breakfast bars

Sunny sesame cherry bars

You will need:

375 mL	salted or unsalted sunflower seeds	1½ c.
375 mL	sesame seeds	1½ c.
250 mL	sun-dried cherries or dried pineapple or apricots, halved	1 c.
250 mL	peanut butter	1 c.
175 mL	honey	¾ c.
125 mL	brown sugar	½ c.
125 mL	wheat germ	½ c.

measuring cups ★ a baking sheet
a sharp knife ★ a medium saucepan
a mixing spoon
a 2 L (8 in. x 8 in.) square pan lined
with wax paper

1. Preheat oven to 300°F (150°C).

2. Spread the sunflower and sesame seeds evenly over the baking sheet. Toast until lightly browned. Turn every 5 minutes. Remove from oven and let cool.

3. Chop the dried cherries in half and set aside.

4. Combine peanut butter, honey and brown sugar in the saucepan. Stir over low heat until blended.

5. Add the cherries and wheat germ and stir.

6. Add the toasted sesame and sunflower seeds. Stir until all dry ingredients are moist.

7. Spoon the mixture in the square pan and pat it down with the back of the spoon until it's smooth.

8. Refrigerate and then serve by cutting into quarters and then cutting each quarter into four bars.

Makes 16 bars

Crispy fruit rolls

You will need:

3 or 4	fruit strips or roll-ups	3 or 4
1 L	miniature marshmallows	4 c.
75 mL	butter	1/3 c.
1 L	crispy rice cereal	4 c.

measuring cups ★ wax paper
a sharp knife ★ a large pot ★ a mixing spoon
a bowl filled with cool water

1. Sprinkle some water on your work area before laying a large sheet of wax paper down, so it doesn't move.

2. Melt the butter and marshmallows in the pot over medium heat. Keep stirring until smooth. Remove from heat.

3. Add the cereal and stir until well coated.

4. Spoon this mixture onto the wax paper. Dip your fingertips in the cool water and rub it over your palms. Work quickly to press the mixture into a rectangle about 3 to 5 cm (1 to 2 in.) thick.

5. Cut and lay the lengths of fruit strips vertically to cover the cereal mixture.

6. Cut the cereal along the edges of the fruit lengths.

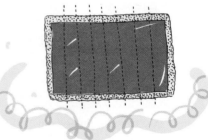

7. Dampen your fingertips slightly and roll up the cereal mixture and fruit lengths like jellyrolls. You should have about 12 to 16 rolls.

8. Refrigerate, then slice each roll in half.

Index